UNCOVERI

UNCOVERING SIN

A gateway to healing and calling

Rosy Fairhurst

First published in Great Britain in 2012

Society for Promoting Christian Knowledge
36 Causton Street
London SW1P 4ST
www.spckpublishing.co.uk

British Library Cataloguing-in-Publication Data
A catalogue record for this book is available from the British Library

ISBN 978–0–281–06879–1
eBook ISBN 978–0–281–06880–7

Typeset by Graphicraft Limited, Hong Kong
First printed in Great Britain by Ashford Colour Press
Subsequently digitally printed in Great Britain

eBook by Graphicraft Limited, Hong Kong

Produced on paper from sustainable forests

This book is dedicated to my father
Alan Marshall Fairhurst
1930–2006
with love

Contents

———◆◆◆———

Acknowledgements	viii
Author's note	ix

Week 1: God's pharmacy 1

1 Strong medicine 1
2 Looking at what harms you to heal you 10

Week 2: Seeing squint? 21

3 In the country of the blind, the one-eyed man is king 21
4 Good and bad squandering 27

Week 3: Binding and loosing 35

5 What sort of a rock? 35
6 The Gadarene swine 44

Week 4: Institutional sin 51

7 The fractal Christ 51
8 Institutional racism 59

Week 5: Darkness into light 67

9 Dazzling darkness 67
10 A life-and-death struggle 75

Week 6: Seeing in the dark 83

11 Opening to the light 83
12 Letting go 90

Week 7: 'Let him easter in us' 97

13 Standing up in the resurrection 97
14 Locked in and locked out? 104

Notes 113

Acknowledgements

I want to thank the communities of St Martin-in-the-Fields, St Paul's Old Ford, the Round Chapel URC Hackney, Ripon College Cuddesdon, St Mary Islington, St Barnabas Homerton and the Hackney Marsh Team, and Wycliffe Hall, Oxford. All of them have nurtured my capacity to teach with their responsive listening and questioning – and I would also like to thank them for putting up, mostly good-humouredly, with my tendency to try to pack too much in when communicating. Some of this book began life as sermons at St Martin-in-the-Fields, where the discipline of trying to satisfy all those enquiring minds and thirsty hearts – and, it should be said, of having to put the text on the internet – is a great incentive.

I'd like to thank Ruth McCurry at SPCK for asking me if I had any material, taking an interest in me as a person, and for the sharpness of her editorial eye.

Author's note

This material can be used for group or individual study. In addition to the questions I have posed at the end of each Week's two chapters, I think there would be much value in each person doing a *lectio divina* – a silent meditation on their own – on one of the Bible readings before any group discussion. All of the sections quote from poems, current events, pictures or other stories, each of which, considered in more depth, would add to the consideration of each theme. Most Lent courses last for five or six weeks. I've put in the sixth Week for use during Holy Week and the seventh because I think it's just too easy to stop when we get to Easter, which is the point at which we can start to live into what it means to be raised with Christ. So please use it, individually or perhaps more powerfully for a final group session in the Easter season.

Week 1
God's pharmacy

---•—•—•—

1 Strong medicine

Genesis 12.1–4

Now the LORD said to Abram, 'Go from your country and your kindred and your father's house to the land that I will show you. I will make of you a great nation, and I will bless you, and make your name great, so that you will be a blessing. I will bless those who bless you, and the one who curses you I will curse; and in you all the families of the earth shall be blessed.'

So Abram went, as the LORD had told him; and Lot went with him. Abram was seventy-five years old when he departed from Haran.

John 3.1–17

Now there was a Pharisee named Nicodemus, a leader of the Jews. He came to Jesus by night and said to him, 'Rabbi, we know that you are a teacher who has come from God; for no one can do these signs that you do apart from the presence of God.' Jesus answered him, 'Very truly, I tell you, no one can see the kingdom of God without being born from above.' Nicodemus said to him, 'How can anyone be born after having grown old? Can one enter a second time into the mother's womb and be born?' Jesus answered, 'Very truly, I tell you, no one can enter the kingdom of God without being born of water and Spirit. What is born of the flesh is flesh, and what is born of the Spirit is spirit. Do not be astonished that I said to you, "You must be born from above." The wind blows where it chooses, and you hear the sound of it, but you do not know where it comes from or where it goes. So it is with everyone who is born of the Spirit.' Nicodemus said to him, 'How can these things be?' Jesus

1

answered him, 'Are you a teacher of Israel, and yet you do not understand these things?

'Very truly, I tell you, we speak of what we know and testify to what we have seen; yet you do not receive our testimony. If I have told you about earthly things and you do not believe, how can you believe if I tell you about heavenly things? No one has ascended into heaven except the one who descended from heaven, the Son of Man. And just as Moses lifted up the serpent in the wilderness, so must the Son of Man be lifted up, that whoever believes in him may have eternal life.

'For God so loved the world that he gave his only Son, so that everyone who believes in him may not perish but may have eternal life.

'Indeed, God did not send the Son into the world to condemn the world, but in order that the world might be saved through him.'

There is a hoary old preaching story in which Mrs Coolidge, wife of US President Calvin Coolidge, asks him about the subject of a sermon he heard: 'Sin', he replied. When asked for a bit more detail about the content he said, 'On the whole he's against it.'

If that had been a contemporary preacher, I'd be tempted to wonder whether he was saying, 'It's a bad thing, we know that – and just look how bad it is', or 'It's a bad idea to think about; we'll only feel terrible, so let's not bother.' Standing where I am, it's the second that's more likely, though it's the sight of how bad it is that has pushed them into turning away. But in fact I want to explore why we need uncover sin, easy though it might be to ignore it when we associate 'sin-talk' with being made to feel worse – more condemned, more blamed – rather than anything potentially liberating.

The purpose of sin-talk

It's impossible to understand the Christian view of sin unless we see it in terms of the whole ecology – that is to say, how it fits together – of the Christian faith. And this is an ecology founded upon God's love, and all our understanding being set in the context of our relationship with God. The trouble with a lot of sin-talk is that it has been taken out of that context. Alistair McFadyen[1] says that the proper function of sin-talk is to turn us to our healing and rescue, to salvation: 'Sin-talk has to serve the communal and personal practices of confession, penitence, intercession, love and forgiveness.'[2] Blame, on the other hand, fixes us there. Even the context of law and sin is covenant – which is relational not contractual. Who would have thought? The way we've tended to think about sin is like ripping Paul's words, 'The wages of sin is death', apart from, 'but the free gift of God is eternal life in Christ Jesus our Lord' (Romans 6.23). We need look no further than the two passages above, among the best known in the whole Bible, to see that this is in fact the way the Bible's sin-talk works.

The Genesis passage, the story of the call of Abraham, comes after 12 chapters telling the story of human sin – first of Adam and Eve and their expulsion from the Garden of Eden after eating the fruit of the tree of the knowledge of good and evil, then the killing of Abel by his brother Cain, the breaking of the commandments, the loss of the capacity to communicate with each other in the story of the Tower of Babel, and the story of Noah, by which stage desperate measures are required to save the sinful world from destruction.

We need to hold on to the fact that we have been given the dove and the rainbow as the sign of the covenant between God and humankind in the Noah story. Now, in this hinge story in Genesis, God turns his attention to show what that covenant of love – God's insatiable desire to bless rather than curse, to rescue humanity rather than condemn – is going to look like in this dire situation. And God does it by focusing on one family, that of Abram and Sarai – one family, whose story and destiny will emerge so that God can show God's love and salvation 'for the nations'. Far from narrowing it down to one family, it will open it right up beyond the people of Israel to all the peoples of the world.

The sin of sin in isolation

Why do we associate sin with cursing and with condemnation? It's partly because the Church has been less than our best self in joining a wider culture that has forgotten the Christian story, and started to think of sin in isolation – as if we were autonomous beings and as if it were a choice between our freedom or God's freedom, without the surrounding story of our relationship with God. As soon as we take sin outside the context of our *relationship* with God, it isn't a Christian understanding any more – because fundamentally that *is* sin, to imagine that we stand autonomously, independently, on our own, removing ourselves from the warmth of God's love. Putting it back into that context reminds us that we are creatures, dependent on God for our very breath, interdependent and connected with the whole of the cosmos.

If I think of the most destructive situations I have encountered recently, they are characterized by a standing apart, by an imagining that there can be no relatedness to the 'other', so that everything is interpreted through a lens of malice and legalism, of the other as dangerous and hostile rather than fundamentally connected. This requires room in which to wonder what the other person's intention was in an action that may have offended us. And it is the consequence of sin, of our separation from the love of God – that we get separated at all levels (from our own bodies even), all our relationships become disordered and disorientated, we lose the capacity to trust and our desires get muddied and misaligned.

Original sin/original blessing

'If you, O Lord, should mark iniquities, Lord, who could stand?' (Psalm 130.3). Answer: no one, of course. The accounts of the Garden of Eden, Cain and Abel and of the Tower of Babel take us into the territory Augustine calls 'original sin'. The way that idea was developed over time has provoked a mighty reaction, articulated most eloquently in Matthew Fox's book, *Original Blessing*.[3] He wants to remind us that God's intention is to bless and not to curse, or as the conclusion of the story from John puts it, Jesus' purpose is not to condemn the world but to save it.

Julian of Norwich makes a beautiful counter-voice within a Church that focuses so much of the time on sin in a way that sees us as already separated from God. She is so clear that this world is one that God made, God loves and God keeps, one that Julian is able to see, with the image of the hazelnut in God's hand as all that is, the interdependence of all things in the light of God's loving gaze. 'It lasteth and ever shall because God loveth it.'[4] Yes, we do need to remember the original blessing and that it extends to the whole of the cosmos, as both Matthew Fox and Julian spell out so eloquently. But Julian knows that we also need to understand that 'sin is behovely'[5] (necessary), and perhaps we need to retrieve a sense of how that is so.

Sin and attachment

I have a friend, a priest and training to be a psychotherapist, who gave her colleagues a set of definitions of Christian concepts in relation to therapeutic terms. She explained original sin in relation to attachment theory – the understanding of how when a child is born, if things go right, a process of attachment takes place between mother and child, and indeed between all the close members of the family and the child. There is a context for love, intimacy, trust, the conditions needed for human beings to thrive. If it fails, if for some reason children aren't able to bond, they will be in big trouble. It's going to be difficult to stay safe because they won't trust their parents, and difficult to form intimate relationships in later life. Depending on what kind of attachment disorder it is, it's going to be difficult for them to stay in relationships at all and might result in all kinds of destructive behaviours.

The clearest example of this in my experience came when I was in touch with a Congolese asylum seeker, Rebecca, and her little son, Monange. Rebecca had been through terrible traumas in the violence in the Congo before escaping to the UK. She got ill and had been admitted to hospital. I was visiting her after she'd been sent home. Quickly it became clear that she was in no fit state to care for her infant son – who with his huge luminous eyes looked like the angel he was named after. I decided there was nothing for it but to take him away and make sure he was looked after that day and maybe longer, until Rebecca was well enough to care for him again. But the really chilling thing was that he didn't cry or protest at all. He'd been surrounded by so much trauma that the normal instinct of an attached child – to scream the house down if someone tried to take him away from his mother – just hadn't had a chance to develop.

When we take our understanding of sin and our behaviour outside the terms of our relationship with a loving God, we are in such a place of separation. We could describe original sin as ways in which we have failed to attach to God but have instead acted out the choice of separation from God – and then from others and indeed the planet. And so we respond with apathy or hostility to God's interventions instead of out of our awareness of being loved. Of course we can't say that this is all our individual fault. We are born into a world where there are many forces that push us towards this separation – this is the nature of original sin. But if we fail to admit our collusion with these forces when we experience their power and impact in our lives and those of others, we are in even bigger trouble.

A big enough diagnosis

Let me give an obvious example at a macro rather than a therapeutic level, because this plays out in groups, organizations, countries and globally, as I shall go on to argue. If we react to our economic crisis by blaming it all on the obvious greed of top bankers, and fail to recognize our collusion (and this applies to the vast majority of us, with the inequities of the current system), whether through property owning, carrying credit cards or benefitting from cheap labour in other parts of the world, 'we deceive ourselves, and the truth is not in us',[6] as the confession says in the Book of Common Prayer. Until we do, we won't start trying to find sustainable alternatives that put us back into right economic relationship with others. This is not about feeling bad, it's about getting to a place where we recognize the extent of the problem and are both open to help to find the solution and ready to accept God's grace in doing so.

Whatever the rights and wrongs of Augustine's understanding of original sin, and of how it has been used and interpreted, there is something very important in his insight that we have to recognize and take accountability for the predicament we are in, whether it is of our own individual making or not. Good psychotherapy doesn't leave patients blaming everyone else for their situation, but it might leave us recognizing our need of a spiritual answer. Good spiritual direction doesn't ignore the extent of the diagnosis of sin – because it is the very thing that clues us in to opening ourselves up to God's saving action. But the diagnosis of sin is about where we have wounded God's love and marred his image in us, rather than blame that keeps us stuck there – that's like inflaming the wound. In my experience, confession has been about recognizing where I've failed to walk in the light of God's love, which is something very different from blame and condemnation. And it has come because I've been put back in touch with God's love at work in my life.

In our passage from John above, Nicodemus' encounter with Jesus begins in the dark. He's used to getting answers, but comes by night as he's not too sure he wants to be seen with Jesus. Jesus tells him that to receive eternal life he needs to recognize that he can't *do* anything by himself to receive it. His spiritual life is not in his control. He must receive it as a gift, being born from above – start to understand his life in terms of relationship with God, not what he can achieve. A gift needs a giver, and Jesus points him forward to the way he will receive this gift – difficult words to hear for someone used to being in control: 'And just as Moses lifted up the serpent in the wilderness, so must the Son of Man be lifted up, that whoever believes in him may have eternal life.'

I'll go on to explore the background of the story of the serpent and the rod from Numbers 21 in the next chapter, but to preview what it shows us, you have to look at what harms you to heal you. The words of Jesus from John's Gospel take us further into this territory. In order to heal our world – for God so loved *the world* – Jesus has first to be lifted up in the place of the full impact of sin. And we have to stay with him there, bringing ourselves, allowing him to show us how we are enmeshed with this sin in the world and just how badly it is harming us and others, before we can receive our healing: healing for ourselves, for our relationships and for our planet. It's strong medicine.

In Lent 2011 we had an opportunity at St Martin-in-the-Fields to take an extended look at what harms us in order to get to what heals us, through the talks given inspired by the *Victim, No Resurrection* crucifix by Liverpudlian artist Terry Duffy, which was on a four-year journey from Liverpool to Jerusalem. The meditations were given by people who'd been at the coalface of the world's violence and suffering, whether as a doctor in Palestinian refugee camps, as was the remarkable orthopaedic surgeon Dr Ang Swee Chai over many years,[7] or through mental illness or personal tragedy in the violent death of a son. If we really believe that God wants to save the world through Christ, how can we avoid facing up to these realities? We are confronted daily by the reality of sin in the world – disease and death and suffering well beyond anyone's individual blame. If our picture of sin isn't big enough to take them in, how are we to understand that this too is part of what God is in the ultimate process of healing and saving?

Questions

1 What are *your* reactions and associations to the word sin?
2 What do you think about the idea that original sin is failure to attach properly to God or to live out of our relationship with God?
3 Do you agree that there is corporate or structural sin as well as individual sin, and that we are tempted to collude with it?
4 What do you think of a definition of sin as 'failure to walk in the light of God's love'?
5 When have you found sin-talk a constructive experience in your life? Does it help to think of sin as a diagnostic rather than a judgement?

2 Looking at what harms you to heal you

Numbers 21.4–9

From Mount Hor they set out by the way to the Red Sea, to go around the land of Edom; but the people became impatient on the way. The people spoke against God and against Moses, 'Why have you brought us up out of Egypt to die in the wilderness? For there is no food and no water, and we detest this miserable food.' Then the LORD sent poisonous serpents among the people, and they bit the people, so that many Israelites died. The people came to Moses and said, 'We have sinned by speaking against the LORD and against you; pray to the LORD to take away the serpents from us.' So Moses prayed for the people. And the LORD said to Moses, 'Make a poisonous serpent, and set it on a pole; and everyone who is bitten shall look at it and live.' So Moses made a serpent of bronze, and put it upon a pole; and whenever a serpent bit someone, that person would look at the serpent of bronze and live.

John 3.14–21

And just as Moses lifted up the serpent in the wilderness, so must the Son of Man be lifted up, that whoever believes in him may have eternal life.

For God so loved the world that he gave his only Son, so that everyone who believes in him may not perish but may have eternal life.

Indeed, God did not send the Son into the world to condemn the world, but in order that the world might be saved through him. Those who believe in him are not condemned; but those who do not believe are condemned already, because they have not believed in the name of the only Son of God. And this is the judgement, that the light has come into the world, and people loved darkness rather than light because their deeds were evil. For all who do evil hate the light and do not come to the light, so that their deeds may not be exposed. But those who do what is true come to the light, so that it may be clearly seen that their deeds have been done in God.

Essence of serpents, pharmacies and strong medicine

I find it hard, as did the Israelites in the desert, to stop staring at the story of the serpent and the rod. And having seen the reaction of the children to it in our C Club (Sunday school) recently, I remain convinced by the power of this strange story in the light of the link John makes with how we are to see the lifting up of Jesus on the cross. Some people try to write it off, claiming that it's more about magic than anything else, but I don't think so.

In the teeth of the Israelites' persistent grumbling in their wilderness wanderings ('God, what are you doing, giving us this awful heavenly food and drink the whole time?' – I'll come back to that phenomenon), God sends a plague of snakes to punish them and then saves them from it by setting up a symbol that looks remarkably like the ancient Greek symbol of Asclepius, the god of healing. It almost beggars belief.

Given Israel's history around graven images, the tendency to want magic rather than faith that we've already seen in the episode with the golden calf and the struggle to leave behind pagan idols, we might ask, 'What exactly does God think God is doing?' Let me explore this. As soon as Moses had left the people to go up the mountain to receive the Ten Commandments, they itched to make idols – couldn't bear not having him physically in their presence to make them feel secure. And so they ended up making a golden calf to which they could ascribe godlike powers, with the added advantage of having a leader who couldn't answer back. That's the thing about magic: it's often really a form of control – quite the opposite of living by faith.

And then just when you think it's safe to go out into the clear light of the gospel, up it comes again. Right in the middle of the most famous Gospel passage of all about the cross, there is the direct reference to the story of the serpent and the rod: 'And just as Moses lifted up the serpent in the wilderness, so must the Son of Man be lifted up.' Is this magic too? Is Jesus setting himself up to be a magic figure who can be called forth as a talisman when he is lifted up on the cross at the crucifixion? The way some people use the symbol of the cross, you might be tempted to think so.

Staring death and life in the face

Let's have a look. There are a few places to go to find out. Let's try a rabbi. Rabbi Arthur Waskow from the Shalom Center has a wonderful piece on this story and the episodes coming before it in the book of Numbers. He explains the instruction to burn red cows 'in red fire, with red wood and red dye in a great cloud of red smoke' as the prescribed ritual to move people from the 'uncleanness' of mourning back into life in community. This state of being turned inward with a particular focus – *tumah*, he tells us – does not really mean impurity or uncleanness as it is usually translated, 'but a spiritual state of laser-beam inward focus (quite different from experiencing holiness in community). *Tumah* might well result from giving birth, touching death, menstruating, having sex.'[8] 'For each of these conditions there was an appropriate time apart and then a ritual to help people move back to life in the community.

If you stare hard into the red, red fire of the burning heifer, Waskow suggests, and then look away (and blink), you will get a blast of green – the green that insists on life afresh. Having queued up at night in Holy Week 2012 to see David Hockney's Yorkshire landscapes at the Royal Academy, I was one to be brought back to life: all those greens, all those vibrant colours, in all their abundant fecundity. I started seeing the spring with Hockney eyes. But it is the Hebrew ritual for death that gives us a basic principle: if we want to be healed, we have to look directly at what harms us. Numbers 20 has Moses speaking to a rock to give the thirsty people water – not perhaps the place you'd think to go first. And then here, in Numbers 21, the cure for snake bites is – to look at a snake. It's the same principle:

the serpent on the rod is the 'serpenty serpent' – essence of serpent – yet it somehow draws the venom of the sting.

Perhaps it's worth reading this story in its own right in a culture today that moves increasingly to funerals without bodies – often for understandable practical reasons – but still leaves the unanswered question about how we can mourn without facing death. We live in a culture where the containing and transforming rituals to help us negotiate life's most powerful transitions have become very thin. This passage in Numbers is from a time when they were absolutely central to the culture.

Pharmakos

These principles help us see the connection between the world of the Hebrews and the Greek idea of *pharmakos*. Just as it is possible to get stuck in mourning and not emerge (you gaze at the red cow and never blink), a drug used in a certain quantity can be a cure but too much is a poison. It gives us the principle of homeopathic medicine that is healthy enough, but as with all kinds of medicine, dangerous if taken in excessive quantities. It's also the principle that gives us the idea of the scapegoat. In ancient Greek religion, the *pharmakos* was a human scapegoat, often someone with a deformity, a slave or a cripple who was expelled from the community – in some cases killed – as a sort of expiation at a time of disaster when purification was needed. On the first day of the *Thargelia*, a festival of Apollo in Athens, two men called *pharmakoi* were actually led out as if to be sacrificed, and some argue were actually sacrificed.

Walter Burkert[9] explores this phenomenon as it occurs in Greek religion, but perhaps the example best known to us is in the story of Theseus and the Minotaur: King Minos of Crete, having defeated the Athenians in battle, ordered that every nine years (every year in some versions), seven of the most handsome and beautiful young men and maidens should be collected and offered to the Minotaur. This creature was half bull, half man, the offspring of his wife Pasiphae's affair with a bull he had stolen from one of the gods. The gods had caused her to fall in love with the bull to punish Minos for his temerity. If youths are ritually offered, as to the Minotaur, we will preserve ourselves from total disaster, the thinking went. Ritual violence saves us from the unmitigated violence of total chaos.

The Hunger Games

I write this shortly after having been implored by my nephew to take him and his sister to see *The Hunger Games*.[10] It's the same principle as the story of the Minotaur: an oppressive regime is demanding the tribute of a young man and young woman from each of its districts, only instead of offering them to the Minotaur, the regime turns it into an extreme reality-TV event where each of the couples must fight each other to the death, and only one will survive. So they're asked to internalize and collude with this mentality that says not only that some must die to save the others, but that life is fundamentally dog eat dog. By killing each other, the tributes make it look as though *they* are the murderers rather than their oppressors – who start to develop all sorts of celebrity angles on the participants as if something quite innocent, life-affirming and entertaining is happening.

The Scapegoat

So we can see that the principle of *pharmakos* is not limited to Greek mythology. René Girard, in his magisterial work *The Scapegoat*,[11] demonstrates very convincingly that this attempt to export blame through violence is stamped all over our world. In the Jewish tradition the goat, part of the ceremonies of Yom Kippur, is sent out into the wilderness to die, taking the blame for the sins of the people. This is memorably portrayed in Holman Hunt's famous painting. Actually he painted two versions – one is in the Lady Lever Art Gallery in Port Sunlight, the other in Manchester City Art Gallery. The Manchester version has a darker goat and a rainbow, a concession to the presence of hope beyond this godforsaken image. Without the rainbow, and possibly even with it, it's very hard to keep looking at this extraordinary rendering of sin outside of the warmth of God's love. That's exactly the point the scapegoat makes.

We know about scapegoating in our culture – it happens all the time. It's so much easier to blame one person and export any sense of our own connectedness to what's going on, whether, in the UK, it's the head of Haringey Children's Services in the 'Baby P' child-abuse case or Fred Goodwin, the former head of the Royal Bank of Scotland, for the financial crisis. We even make paedophiles the sole focus of our outrage on behalf of children when it's clear there are multiple ways and levels in which, as a society, we fail our children.

Pharmacy

The artist Damien Hirst came to prominence with an installation called *Pharmacy*. In this and other works he explores our culture's obsession with the power of drugs as if they could defend us from our helplessness against death. For the millennium, I was involved in a great project called 'Art in Sacred Spaces', which displayed contemporary artwork in different worship spaces around the East End of London, and we were going to display Hirst's *The Last Supper* at St Mary Islington, where I was based. Where stations of the cross might be hung, he had images of pharmaceutical packets bearing, instead of the Latinate titles of drugs, basic generic food names like 'sausages'. It reminded me of the discarded needles and packets sometimes left in the graveyard, and provoked by far the best conversation we ever had in my time at St Mary's about the 'true food' of Christ's body and blood and life-giving power present in Communion. And it did so because we could see so starkly what poor substitutes our culture tries to put in its place. But there was strong opposition to its going ahead, and in the end we showed an appliquéd blanket by Tracey Emin, made in conjunction with local schoolchildren, called *Tell Me Something Beautiful*. It was a truly wonderful thing to explain the symbols of the sanctuary to lots of schoolchildren who had never been into church before and who saw their own work displayed in what was clearly the most special part of the church. But it's also true that it's easier to look at something beautiful than to look at what harms you to heal you. Sometimes we have to look at the red before we can see the green, force ourselves to stare at the godforsaken goat, confront the ersatz substitute before we can see the real and the true and the beautiful again.

The divine BMA code

And so we return to the serpent and rod. Of course, the British Medical Association (BMA) shares the sign of the serpent and the rod with Asclepius, the Greek god of healing, as well as with this scene from Numbers in the Bible – we've taken it deeply into our culture as a sign of healing. In Greek mythology Asclepius was brought up by Chiron the centaur, the original wounded healer who, having lived out of his human intellectual side as a teacher, had to come to terms with his horse-half after he was shot by an arrow and left with a terrible wound. That's what drove him to learn the arts of medicine from herbs as he ventured out from the sanctuary of his cave. He then taught these skills to Asclepius. He had to come to terms with his creatureliness. As the son of a Titan he was immortal, but he was content to exchange his immortality with Prometheus to escape his chronic pain. Prometheus, on the other hand, was left to endure his torment for ever.

Asclepius in turn became the most famous healer of all and the god of healing and medicine in the pantheon, but was then punished by the gods for raising Hippolytus from the dead and accepting gold for it. He broke the divine BMA code. (Every doctor has to abide by the Code of Practice that enshrines the ethical values of practising medicine. To break them is to risk being struck off the list of recognized medical practitioners.) So resonances of mortality, immortality, death and resurrection abound between the Greek myths and in this story of the serpent and the rod. They give us fresh resources to understand the newness of the death and resurrection of Christ.

Of course, the Israelites knew nothing of Greek mythology, but the idea that God chose to send a plague of serpents had definite associations for them. Satan the tester, who had whispered in their ear suggesting they take an autonomous view of their own power and desires (and rail in different ways against God's gracious provision), literally came back to bite them.

Faith and magic

Why on earth should the Israelites be complaining when God gives them bread from heaven and water from the rock? Perhaps because it's out of their control, they haven't made it for themselves, they're not in charge. Whereas *magic* may present us with the illusion of potency, instant power and autonomy, the life of faith does the reverse, reminding us of our dependence and asking us often simply to take the next step and learn to trust.

When we're in freefall – a bit as we are in the global financial system, which makes any idea about permanent financial security unrealistic for all of us – it is a gift to learn to live by faith. As we have seen the movement from the 'magic' of the conjuring of imaginary money for speculation to a situation where lots of us are now forced to wrestle afresh with what it might mean to live by faith in the area of our finances, we have become connected to the vast majority of the world's population as well as, potentially, to God. In any case, when the Israelites looked up at the serpent on the rod, they were healed of their snake bites. Is it the act of faith in looking up; is it a touch of *pharmakos*?

What can we tell from linking this event with the lifting up of Jesus on the cross? It warns us of the dangers of idolizing the cross. Just as the serpent on the rod got made into an idol that brought magical thinking rather than faith and recalls to us the constant human temptation towards scapegoating, so does the cross. When this passage in John – when theories of the cross – are used as a bludgeon to say who's in and who's out, to condemn people and send them to outer darkness, it becomes exactly what Jesus offers to save us from.

Walking in the light

John is absolutely clear: the raising up of the Son on the cross is not to condemn the world 'but in order that the world might be saved through him'. If we dare to look at Jesus lifted up on the cross – yes, we'll see a scapegoat *and* something of our own part in sending him there through our sin and blaming others for what we can't bear to see in ourselves. But we'll see something else. Instead of a God who accepts our ritual sacrifices to ward off further violence and destruction, as we've come to expect from the behaviour of gods in the past, God gives his own Son to stop the slaughter. Jesus becomes the true scapegoat who releases us from the endless cycle of sacrificial violence.

We might feel that the danger of bringing things into the light is that we'll be condemned, exposed. No, says John – quite the reverse:

> Those who believe in him are not condemned; but those who do not believe are condemned already, because they have not believed in the name of the only Son of God. And this is the judgement, that the light has come into the world, and people loved darkness rather than light because their deeds were evil.
>
> (John 3.18–19)

The safest place to bring things is into the light – where the poison can be drawn. It's keeping them in the dark that's dangerous. That's where the microbes fester – that's where we consign ourselves to prison and poison.

The nature of judgement

Jesus does not come to judge – yet when we refuse his offer we leave ourselves exposed to our own snake bites because they stand revealed in the presence and light of the holy one. The cross is like a lightning rod: in it sin's force and poison are drawn and grounded because of the action of Jesus. He goes to the place of the scapegoat, but because he is untainted by that poison, it cannot ultimately harm him. This is no magical object; nor is it a cruel sacrifice by a capricious God. The Son of Man is compared to the serpent. Do we see the horror of the crucifixion as we look right into it, beholding the sin and destructiveness of ourselves and our world? Do we get stuck there or do we, as with the red-cow ritual, close our eyes and open them again to see the healing and green new resurrection life offered there? Can we keep our eyes fixed on the cross, the point of contradiction, and find ourselves healed instead of judged?

Questions

1 *Pharmakos* – looking at what harms you to heal you. What personal experience have you had of this? Do you recognize it as part of the experience of looking at Christ on the cross?

2 How do you recognize the presence of scapegoats in society? Where have you seen them in your working, family and even church lives? (You might want to look at the Holman Hunt pictures of the scapegoat, which you can view online.)

3 What can we learn from the different Greek myths explored if we consider them in relation to our Christian understanding of sin and salvation?

4 What is the difference between faith and magic? When can we recognize a desire for magic in our own faith journey?

5 How does this study challenge your view of the atonement? What happened on the cross?

Week 2
Seeing squint?

---

3 In the country of the blind,
the one-eyed man is king

Mark 9.38–50

John said to him, 'Teacher, we saw someone casting out demons in your name, and we tried to stop him, because he was not following us.' But Jesus said, 'Do not stop him; for no one who does a deed of power in my name will be able soon afterwards to speak evil of me. Whoever is not against us is for us. For truly I tell you, whoever gives you a cup of water to drink because you bear the name of Christ will by no means lose the reward.

'If any of you put a stumbling-block before one of these little ones who believe in me, it would be better for you if a great millstone were hung around your neck and you were thrown into the sea. If your hand causes you to stumble, cut it off; it is better for you to enter life maimed than to have two hands and to go to hell, to the unquenchable fire. And if your foot causes you to stumble, cut it off; it is better for you to enter life lame than to have two feet and to be thrown into hell. And if your eye causes you to stumble, tear it out; it is better for you to enter the kingdom of God with one eye than to have two eyes and to be thrown into hell, where their worm never dies, and the fire is never quenched.

'For everyone will be salted with fire. Salt is good; but if salt has lost its saltiness, how can you season it? Have salt in yourselves, and be at peace with one another.'

Steve Bell had a very striking cartoon in *The Guardian* in September 2010. It had US President Barack Obama sitting in the Oval Office speaking to the nation saying, 'He's a blind, fat, naughty world statesman of the year', with the then UK Prime Minister

Gordon Brown in his 'superstatesman' outfit turned to the naughty corner. It was in the context of Brown's visit to New York (after being given a 'World Statesman of the Year' accolade, before the Copenhagen Climate Change conference, the alleged 'snubbing' of his requests to meet one-to-one with Obama and the press's putting the question of his health in the public domain).

It made me laugh, but then I started reading the furore in the responses (online) about whether this is sick – just taking advantage of the gossip about whether Brown *was* turning blind in his good eye; not to mention being fattist; probably childrenist too. Then I came across this response: 'In the country of the blind, the one-eyed man is king', and thought, 'That's it!' Somehow it seemed to connect this string of apparently random – and very difficult – sayings Mark has thrown together. Let's see if it does for you.

Clearly the most obvious connection is with the section about the chopping off of the parts of our body that cause us to stumble. Is Jesus commending the judicial practice of some Islamic states as a role model here for the Christian community? When does having one eye become an advantage?

I think there are connections to be made here with questions of leadership and who we're following, and, in our well-'spun' world, about brand protection and brand purity. I think there's something in here too about how we learn to spot the real scandals.

Brand protection

'Teacher, we saw someone casting out demons in your name, and we tried to stop him, because he was not following us [not one of us].' It's not, you will note, that these people didn't do the deeds in Jesus' name. In fact they'd done the very things Jesus had been so frustrated with his inner group for not having the faith to accomplish.

They may be people right on the edge of church, they may be people from another part(y) of it, but if they're truly connected with the same source – Jesus – and owning that, then they're not going to disavow him afterwards, are they? And if they are, it will soon become obvious – surely? Jesus seems to be telling the disciples to be a bit less worried about their brand protection. The good from 'outside' must be affirmed, but on the other hand, we must be incredibly careful about brand purity – if there's bad on the 'inside', we must cut it out.

An unnamed professor of theology once said, 'Whenever you want to draw lines in order to mark who is outside the kingdom and who is inside, always remember: Jesus is on the other side of the line! Jesus is always with the outsiders!'

Spotting the real scandals

When Jesus then goes on to talk about stumbling blocks and little ones, I don't know about you, but I immediately think 'child abuse'. Jesus has just brought the little child in and said the disciples must be like this to enter the kingdom.

The word for stumbling block is the word to *scandalize*. To scandalize can be to entrap or to cause anger and shock in society. Too often we distance the one from the other. If we look at the Church's response to child abuse, often the first step has been to cover it up, allowing further entrapment, and to continue to act as if angry and shocked by the issue as a whole. Actually, stopping the harm of the little ones is the first priority before such expressions of anger and shock at the scandals of the world can be taken seriously and seen as congruent again.

Of course, 'little ones' aren't only children. They are any who are poor, marginalized, at risk in the body of society or living on the edge.

In the country of the blind, the one-eyed man is king

So it's in this light that we need to look at these fierce words about cutting off limbs. No, I don't think it's literal, but I think Jesus is telling us that to stay with him we have to keep turning away from what causes us, and others through us, to stumble;

what clouds our clear vision of the inclusion of the kingdom. So we have to take sin seriously, and we have to turn away from it.

Barack Obama connects himself with Christian values and so holds himself accountable for living and acting by this standard. Is criticism of the regime allowed? Who takes action on it when necessary? Who listens to the voices of the 'little ones'? What keeps them safe in the face of all the louder cries of the 'top guns'?

Isn't the description of hell Jesus paints in this picture what gets played out in totalitarian regimes (whether countries or churches), sometimes only too literally? The Valley of Hinnom, which is referred to in 2 Kings 23.10, was one of the two principal valleys surrounding ancient Jerusalem. In this place apostate Hebrews and Baal worshippers sacrificed their children by fire. In the New Testament it is called Gehenna and becomes a generic term for the destination of the wicked. So it was a place where worship had been traduced in the most appalling ways. If some cutting off isn't done metaphorically, we end up with the silos of limbs that go with the endgame of totalitarian regimes – Nazism, Cambodia, the Lord's Resistance Army – or the baskets of hands cut off workers from King Leopold's rubber plantations in the Belgian Congo that were used to terrorize the workforce into higher production.

I got interested in the Democratic Republic of Congo (DRC), formerly the Belgian Congo, partly through meeting Rebecca and Monange, whom I spoke about in Chapter 1, and partly through reading *The Poisonwood Bible*, the magnificent novel by Barbara Kingsolver,[1] while I was visiting Burkina Faso, West Africa. I kept hearing about how few resources Burkina Faso had, and I saw with my own eyes how the already thin land of the Sahel on which it's placed is being alarmingly eroded by climate change. But it's also true that Burkina Faso has diamond mines – it's just that most of the profit from them doesn't reach the people. Compared to the history of the

DRC, however, Burkina Faso is blessed. If you want to read an extended meditation on what hell on earth can look like, and the consequences of failing to cut out the eyes that offend us (whether as Christian ministers or colonizing powers), read not only *The Poisonwood Bible* but also *King Leopold's Ghost*[2] by Adam Hochschild. It's a very sobering experience.

So sometimes to be one-eyed is good, if it means we realize where we're damaged and what we're going to do to prevent the harm spreading. It's like agreeing to have an operation for a cancer to be removed. That's a really mature thing to do – but incredibly hard. But such *metanoia*, such turning away, is never easy, always strong medicine, because it's so important for us to preserve our illusions, our images of being whole and perfect – because of our twisted view of brand purity, in fact.

Brand purity

'Salt is good; but if salt has lost its saltiness, how can you season it?' Pure sodium chloride can't lose its saltiness, but if it starts as impure, part of a solution, it can. As I have already suggested, Jesus seems here to rate brand purity very highly. What might the hallmarks of a Christian community be? Serving the poor? Encouraging the 'little ones' in faith? Welcoming all who act and speak 'in Jesus' name' (that is, being in partnership rather than competition with other Christian groups)? But if there was one word we'd want to see in the list of most referenced qualities from our focus groups it would be 'forgiveness'. How else are we to live with our weaknesses and stay in communion with others (and their weaknesses), and work through all our conflicts? And how else will we be able to model that to a world that so desperately needs reconciling?

Questions

1 Brand protection – Can we think of times when we're tempted to be overly protective of our 'brand' in our church life or in our working or family lives?

2 In the country of the blind, the one-eyed man is king – How do you understand this saying? Where can you see it in practice?

3 Spotting the real scandals – What, from your perspective, are the real scandals going on in society that tend to get obscured by the ones that grab the headlines?

4 Brand purity – What could we do to attend to the brand purity of our own church, and whatever other brand we represent or help produce?

5 How do you make sense of Jesus' language about hell?

4 Good and bad squandering

Luke 16.1–13

Then Jesus said to the disciples, 'There was a rich man who had a manager, and charges were brought to him that this man was squandering his property. So he summoned him and said to him, "What is this that I hear about you? Give me an account of your management, because you cannot be my manager any longer." Then the manager said to himself, "What will I do, now that my master is taking the position away from me? I am not strong enough to dig, and I am ashamed to beg. I have decided what to do so that, when I am dismissed as manager, people may welcome me into their homes." So, summoning his master's debtors one by one, he asked the first, "How much do you owe my master?" He answered, "A hundred jugs of olive oil." He said to him, "Take your bill, sit down quickly, and make it fifty." Then he asked another, "And how much do you owe?" He replied, "A hundred containers of wheat." He said to him, "Take your bill and make it eighty." And his master commended the dishonest manager because he had acted shrewdly; for the children of this age are more shrewd in dealing with their own generation than are the children of light. And I tell you, make friends for yourselves by means of dishonest wealth so that when it is gone, they may welcome you into the eternal homes.

'Whoever is faithful in a very little is faithful also in much; and whoever is dishonest in a very little is dishonest also in much. If then you have not been faithful with the dishonest wealth, who will entrust to you the true riches? And if you have not been faithful with what belongs to another, who will give you what is your own? No slave can serve two masters; for a slave will either hate the one and love the other, or be devoted to the one and despise the other. You cannot serve God and wealth.'

Sometimes Jesus used hyperbole to make his point, as in talking about cutting off hands and cutting out eyes. In the parables, Jesus seems intent on prising our assumptions open for long enough, with his teasing, surprising 'surely not' stories, to allow for the possibility of a real change of heart, mind and will. He makes us work, and he doesn't let us settle into one certain answer – and we have to keep returning to the story in new contexts that provoke new understandings.

But the need for a real change of heart, mind and will is where the last chapter led us. And this story – of the unjust steward – gets us to grapple with the paradigm shift.

Puncturing certainties

Just as theatre, film and literature ask us to suspend disbelief at the play-acting to access truth that's easier to see because it's at one remove, so do Jesus' parables. They challenge our sense of right and wrong so that we can see where we've laid down the lines with too much certainty – and whenever we do that we reduce the big picture of the kingdom to a close-up of a tiny part of the whole, which makes little sense taken on its own. So what are the certainties punctured by this particular parable?

What we have, first of all, is a steward who appears to confuse his role with that of his boss. The accusation is that he's been squandering his boss's resources. 'Squandering' is an interesting word, the same one that's been used of the Prodigal Son's squandering of his father's inheritance (in the previous chapter of Luke). But it's worse in a way: these aren't the steward's resources to squander, not even his legal inheritance.

To whom is Jesus addressing his story? The answer is, his disciples – the very people he's entrusting with becoming stewards of his spiritual message. 'Give me an accounting of your management, for you cannot be my manager any longer.' The unjust steward is called to account – sacked. Under pressure of facing this unpalatable and inconvenient truth, he takes stock of his position. What's going to happen to him now?

As it stands, it's not as if the people he's been collecting rents from are going to welcome him with open arms – he has after all been charging them extortionate and crippling sums of money. Is that so he can make his cut? Is it because the landowner has insisted? Whatever the reason, he takes the radical step of slashing the amounts – knocking a few noughts off the invoices – to make them sizes people can afford to pay so that they can be freed from their debt.

Prudence

'What a shrewd move!' the master responds. And the word is the one we get 'prudence' from, the word so beloved of Gordon Brown when he was UK chancellor and prime minister. It's prudent in this case because by slashing the debt, the steward is putting himself back in the good books of all these people, whose help and hospitality he will need if he's not strong enough to dig and too ashamed to beg. And it's prudent because he's creating the scenario that when the master returns to collect his money he'll find himself greeted like a hero for transforming these people's lives and releasing them from oppression – whereas before he would probably have been greeted with joyless deference and suppressed resentment.

What's the master to do? Should he say, 'The deal's off; it's all a scam; you're as you were with the debts' and make himself three times as unpopular as before and possibly cause a riot? Or should he 'go with the flow' and accept his new role as Mr Popular? I know which one I'd go for – and I think I might give the steward his job back while I was about it.

Forgiveness

So what is this story about? The most blindingly obvious reading is that it's about forgiveness, yet you wouldn't know that if you looked at the bulk of interpretations in the tradition. It's even clearer if we remember that it comes in the Gospel of Luke, right after the parables of the lost sheep, lost coin and lost son; in the Gospel whose version of the Lord's Prayer literally says, 'Forgive us our sins as we forgive our debtors' – deliberately muddling and equating our spiritual forgiveness with the way we handle economic debtors. It's as though Jesus is saying, 'FORGIVE. Forgive it all. Forgive it now. Forgive it for any reason you want, or for no reason at all.'[3]

You may not find it within you to forgive from the heart, but ultimately, unforgiveness is like a poison that stays with the person in whose power forgiveness lies. That may not seem fair, it may seem like adding insult to injury, but it's true.

Seeking forgiveness

I found myself compelled to try to understand what this parable had to say to us when the terrible history of sexual abuse within the Catholic Church was brought right into the harsh daylight of public life through the Pope's visit in 2010 and the 'Protest the Pope' march that came through Trafalgar Square the day he was in London that September. This history of abuse was named, right in the spiritual heart of the Catholic institution through the Pope's words in the context of his homily at Westminster Cathedral. The homily was for the dedication of the Cathedral to the Most Precious Blood of Jesus, and the Pope took the opportunity to bring this issue to the cross. It was followed by the most profound and extended silence by the whole congregation – a silence I understood to involve a reconnecting, with compassion and shame, with the truth of the situation for the victims and with those implicated in the abuse, through bringing the whole knotted tangle to the place of justice, forgiveness and healing.

But the question remains from the voice of 'Protest the Pope': When will the Church acknowledge that this abuse did not just happen but was systematically covered up and therefore allowed to go on, to protect the institution of the Church rather than the victims? There is more to acknowledge and name for forgiveness to happen, they're saying. The steward needs to look deeper into his own injustice.

I found myself wrestling with this injunction to forgive when I attended a course run by Christian Survivors of Sexual Abuse – a largely Catholic organization – as a curate of an inner-city church, where at one point I reckoned that at least one in eight of the core congregation had spoken of sexual abuse in their experience, mostly in family contexts.

The leader of that course, herself a survivor, would repeatedly say, 'Don't tell survivors to forgive.' Before you forgive you have to have got to the place where you can feel the anger and the outrage that comes from some kind of sense of self rather than just the shame and the guilt. Never tell a survivor they have to forgive, she would insist. Can we reconcile these two positions?

'For the children of this age are more shrewd in dealing with their own generation than are the children of light.' Here is Jesus' punchline to the parable. He wants us to think about how this parable works in our generation. Does this interpretation, this call to forgive, have value in our own generation?

Watching the astonishing fanfare and the singing of 'Tu es Petrus' that greeted the arrival of the Pope in the Cathedral, I couldn't help remembering how the Pope is understood – as the descendant of Peter, who was given authority for the binding and loosing of sins. And on this authority his role is founded – an authority he took on this trip and has taken more widely in his ministry to call the secular West back to a commitment to truth in the face of moral relativism.

I heard the Pope remind the people of their priestly vocation. I put this together with the reminder I had reading Lucy Winkett's article in *The Tablet* about what she would say if she had five minutes with the Pope. She took the opportunity to talk about the ordination of women and to remember that for a lot of women there has to be a process of finding themselves in feeling and knowing their dignity and self-worth and beloved-ness, a true sense of self, before they can lose themselves for the sake of the gospel.

This is one of the most serious challenges of Christian feminism, one I believe was originally made by Valerie Saiving back in 1960, in her article 'The Human Situation: A Feminine View'.[4]

The crux of Saiving's argument is that the focus on pride, characteristic of traditional Christian interpretations of sin, reflects male experience in a way that does not match the experience of most, if not all, women, who are much more likely to be prone to 'triviality, distractibility, and diffuseness; lack of an organizing centre or focus; dependence on others for one's self-definition; tolerance at the expense of standards of excellence . . . in short, underdevelopment or negation of the Self'. Of course, the impact of sexual abuse magnifies these issues for many survivors, and not just women: it is all part of why it is so hard for them to forgive.

Finding authority to forgive

The key thing here is that this passage assumes *all* have the authority to forgive – an authority that comes from being God's steward, Jesus' followers and part of a priestly people. The steward isn't condemned for forgiving what under strict accounting is not his to forgive: he is commended. The priest and the bishop are to *represent* the authority given to forgive on behalf of the people, not to take it away from them. And the authority given is to forgive, not to take God's accounting into our own hands.

So for the survivors of sexual abuse, the radical hope in this story of the unjust steward is that there can be a process of dis-covering their own agency, their own authority – a place from which to forgive. Sometimes it feels as though the experience of forgiving something that has gone very deep is a bit like removing layer after layer of an onion: you forgive all you can and then find there is more – with tears. So it is a slow and painful process of healing, though often significantly accelerated when those involved in committing the sin can admit it. And we will know when that authority has been discovered and when healing has been found, because it is then possible for the sins to be forgiven.

Bad squandering and good squandering

This is also a parable about being forgiven – the two always go hand in hand in the Gospels. It's a parable that reasserts some key principles in Luke's understanding of the divine economy. There's bad squandering, for which, like the Prodigal Son, we have to come in repentance and hope that God will squander his love rather than call us to account. But there's also good squandering, such as when the shepherd squanders the ninety-nine sheep to go in search of the one lost one, or when the sower squanders the seed on all sorts of unpromising as well as fertile ground. This good squandering, of generosity or grace, is the hallmark of divine economics. We have to leave the accounting up to God so that we avoid hoarding resentment or stockpiling the treasure out of the reach of those who need it.

We need to understand that the commodity of 'unrighteous mammon' – of money abused as a personal insurance policy in a world of fear and lack – needs to be transformed into the good gift of God's abundance, which if squandered rightly can begin to reconnect the rich with the poor, the victims with the perpetrators, in a just and joyful community.

Questions

(There may well be people in the group who have suffered from sexual abuse directly or indirectly, so please tread very sensitively if and when you discuss this issue.)

1 Bad squandering and good squandering – explore further the difference between the two.

2 What do you do when you're not ready or able to forgive someone?
3 How do you find it helpful to confess your sins? Do you ever make a formal confession? Talk to a friend? What else do you do?
4 What do you think of Valerie Saiving's point about the different forms sin can take? Are there any other ones not usually covered that start coming to mind?

Week 3
Binding and loosing

---

5 What sort of a rock?

Isaiah 51.1–2a

> Listen to me, you that pursue righteousness,
> you that seek the LORD.
> Look to the rock from which you were hewn,
> and to the quarry from which you were dug.
> Look to Abraham your father
> and to Sarah who bore you.

Matthew 16.13–20

Now when Jesus came into the district of Caesarea Philippi, he asked his disciples, 'Who do people say that the Son of Man is?' And they said, 'Some say John the Baptist, but others Elijah, and still others Jeremiah or one of the prophets.' He said to them, 'But who do you say that I am?' Simon Peter answered, 'You are the Messiah, the Son of the living God.' And Jesus answered him, 'Blessed are you, Simon son of Jonah! For flesh and blood has not revealed this to you, but my Father in heaven. And I tell you, you are Peter, and on this rock I will build my church, and the gates of Hades will not prevail against it. I will give you the keys of the kingdom of heaven, and whatever you bind on earth will be bound in heaven, and whatever you loose on earth will be loosed in heaven.' Then he sternly ordered the disciples not to tell anyone that he was the Messiah.

From that time on, Jesus began to show his disciples that he must go to Jerusalem and undergo great suffering at the hands of the elders and chief priests and scribes, and be killed, and on the third day be raised. And Peter took him aside and began to rebuke him, saying, 'God forbid it, Lord! This must never happen to you.' But he turned and said to Peter, 'Get behind me, Satan! You are a stumbling-block to me; for you are setting your mind not on divine things but on human things.'

What sort of a rock is this? It's an interesting question at a time when our society is looking around and desperately seeking something to stand on, something to cling to. At the time of writing, in 2012, we can see the flaws in our society, materialism and greed, as institutionalized in our banking system and as exposed by the parliamentary-expenses scandal, mirrored by the ugly criminality of looting by those who don't have such sophisticated means at their disposal and who are galled by seeing things dangled out of their reach. We see the integrity of the police, government and media rocked by the phone-hacking scandal. We see the financial systems of the world in panic, putting our own security into doubt. And meanwhile people starve in the Horn of Africa, and violent struggles for and against freedom continue around the world.

Where is the rock on which we can stand at such a time? We have already been thinking about the role claimed for the Pope as Peter's successor, and yet the moral authority of the Catholic Church, as we have already considered, is compromised by the abuse scandals and cover-ups that have rocked it around the world. Of course, we know that other parts of the Church are not immune from their own struggles, centring for the Anglicans at the moment, perhaps, on what it is going to bind and what it is going to loose in terms of authority and sexuality. I'll return to this story in Week 4.

This passage is often split apart from the section, immediately afterwards, when Peter goes 'from hero to zero' in his abject failure to understand the nature of what Jesus must go through to fulfil his ministry, even though he's identified it so clearly here as being the way to the cross. Jesus has prophesied that he must suffer, be killed and rise, and Peter blurts out,

'God forbid, Lord. This shall never happen to you', provoking Jesus to turn and say 'Get behind me, Satan! You are a hindrance to me; for you are not on the side of God, but of human beings.' But isn't this bit of lectionary-snipping simply indicative of the constant human tendency to split – to want to make heroes and villains but to keep from recognizing that they belong within the same human being, just as it is with us ourselves?

The joy of being wrong

There's an excellent book called *The Joy of Being Wrong* by James Alison[1] – and *that's* what Peter will need to discover. What he has to learn, after the revelation of this insight into Jesus' identity, is that to inhabit fully what it means, he has to find the *joy of being wrong* greater than the *thrill of being right.* Remember that even Jesus had to experience the joy of being wrong to overcome his cultural lenses and move from seeing the Syro-Phoenician woman who pleaded with him to heal her daughter as a 'dog' (Mark 7.24–30) – I'll return to this story later.

Peter, the rock, on the other hand, gets it wrong repeatedly. It was the joy of being wrong that released his radical compassion and the fullness of his ministry. Peter is going to have to learn that 'right doctrine' is only part of the story.

Trust and orthodoxy – the case of Constantine

Interestingly, Matthew doesn't seem to link faith with credal confession, the backbone of 'right doctrine'. Both Peter's little faith and the Canaanite woman's (as she is called in Matthew's version of the Syro-Phoenician woman's story in 15.21–28) great faith are linked to *trust*, not orthodoxy. Good call. We have too much evidence of what happens when credal confession – saying the 'right' words as the touchstone of belief – gets separated from trust and starts to be used as a defence of empire and power, whether political or ecclesiastical, or as a weapon to justify violence. Let's not forget the Emperor Constantine.

This was the man who underwrote the Council of Nicaea, which produced the Nicene Creed that many churches around the world still say on most Sundays. This gave him the chance to decide which bishops got invited and the final say on agreed statements. Legend has it that the statement that the Son is of 'one substance' or 'one Being' with the Father came from him. And yet this is the same man who wasn't baptized until his deathbed and who continued to build and worship in temples to Sol Invictus, the all-conquering sun-god his ancestors had worshipped.

Sarah Dylan Breuer, to whom I owe this (and many other) insights, says this:

> Constantine was right on the question of Jesus' titles. Unfortunately, he was wrong on the far more important question of Jesus' character, and the character of the god who is Jesus' Father. Constantine grew up worshipping a god who was all about power, and specifically the power that would help him become powerful, victorious in battle, supreme over his enemies. And he never stopped worshipping that god. He never stopped worshipping power. And so Constantine could confess that Jesus is the only-begotten Son of God, and could put an empty throne next to his so he could claim to rule as Jesus' agent, and still murder his children if they posed a threat to his power. He turned Jesus' name, Jesus' God, and even Jesus' cross, into symbols by which he hoped to conquer and rule.[2]

And this had a lasting impact on the role of the institutional Church, taking it far from the *ekklesia*, the community of people called out from their cultures, which Jesus was calling into being, into the era of Christendom, when Church was inseparable from political power.

Binding and loosing

'Binding and loosing' is a phrase that today perhaps is most associated with a very particular use of the term in some parts of the Church with relation to exorcism. Now that may be one area the concept relates to, though I don't think in any formulaic or magical or controlling way, and when we look at the incident of the Gadarene swine later on we may see how. But this is a term that has more to do with authority and interpretation.

The Jewish community used it to talk about the way rabbis were interpreting the law, for example, 'If a man made a vow to abstain from milk, he is loosed (with respect to) whey. Rabbi Yosi binds it . . . If a man made a vow to abstain from meat, he is loosed (with respect to) broth (in which it was cooked) . . . (but) Rabbi Judah binds it.'[3] Matthew was writing to a largely Jewish community who would recognize this kind of usage. He uses the terms together only twice, in this passage and in 18.1, when talking about church discipline and excommunicating members of the community. But he uses it more broadly, for example in 5.31–2, when Jesus 'binds' divorce, except for unfaithfulness, where he looses it; in 12.9–14 when he looses healing on the Sabbath, where all work has been bound before; and in 15.17–19 when Jesus implies that he is both loosing the law by coming to fulfil it, and binding because he won't remove a jot or tittle from it.

The vexed question of how to interpret Jesus' words about divorce – and the other questions about interpretation of biblical texts in relation to areas Jesus was silent about, such as homosexuality – illustrates that we are quite confused in practice as to what kind of authority we're talking about that can bind and loose. Matthew makes it clear that true spiritual authority doesn't come from purity of doctrine alone. From the evidence of Jesus' action in Peter's life, and many others', it becomes clear that spiritual authority comes from the whole experience of revelation, forgiveness and faith – and that as soon as we try to take our stand on less than the whole of this experience, we seem to enter the territory of human judgement and of loosing our moorings from the gift and promise of God. To see why Peter becomes a figure of spiritual authority, we have to look at the whole of his story – sinking in the sea because of his lack of faith (Matthew 14.22–33), cutting the slave's ear off because of his lack of understanding (John 18.10–11), betraying Jesus because of his lack of courage (Luke 22.54–62) and then being restored from all these things to a relationship of deepened love and trust (John 21.15–19).

The Church has gone a long way down the line of separating off doctrinal correctness in the way this account of Peter has been used: it has led to the idea of papal infallibility; to a quality of argument about difference in our own Church that too often assumes that this is the only factor in discerning truth in whatever area we are arguing about. I think we need to read this passage in terms of Peter as the representative disciple who stands for all of us and how we take up our authority to bind and loose. This takes us into the territory of how we find our authority to forgive, how to liberate and how to resist evil.

Jesus tells some startling parables on the subject, and we can add to that of the unjust steward from the last chapter the story of the unforgiving servant (Matthew 18.23–35) who's been released from his huge debt by his master but can't forgive the much smaller debt he is owed himself, and gets cast out as a result. This parable comes directly after Peter has asked the question, 'Lord, how often shall my brother sin against me and I forgive him?', which in turn follows Matthew's other 'binding and loosing' passage, in the context of a painful question of church discipline. These parables raise some very challenging questions about the nature of judgement.

They also open up the area of how we can participate in our own destructive *binding* – how not forgiving others, refusing to live in the world of forgiveness, causes us to become bound up in that world of unforgiveness ourselves. On the other hand, what happens when we forgive someone is that we bind an experience of the character of God into their hearts, and into our lives, and we loose them, we free them from guilt and shame and ourselves from our resentment.[4] And the effect of that constructing binding is to liberate, to loose.

Perhaps we tend to think more of binding in its negative terms of what is forbidden by religious authority, where people feel thrown into outer darkness. Sometimes people are left bearing very heavy loads when that human judgement happens inappropriately – in a way that presumes to speak for the divine judgement. The difference is that in the end divine judgement, as expressed on the cross, looses rather than binds.

We should remember, however, to whom Matthew is writing (conservative Jews), and that here he is, setting up Peter as the one who's been explicitly authorized by Jesus to bind and loose – Peter, the very person who received the revelation about the inclusion of the Gentiles. Matthew is doing some loosing here himself, as well as Peter, in authorizing the inclusion of the Gentiles into the infant Church through the way he relates the authorization of Peter. I'll say more about that issue when we return to the story of the Canaanite woman.

'Who do you say that I am?'

Jesus asks Peter how he understands his authority. 'Who do you say that the fully human one (the Son of Man) is?' What kind of authority are you following?

Why does he ask him? Of course, if we are followers, then how we understand our own identity, the way we understand our own authority to bind and loose, depends on how we understand our leader's authority. And we need the challenge, like Peter, of how and where we are prepared to confess Christ – to say who he is to us. It's not even just about what we understand by 'Son of God' – a massive question in itself to keep on wrestling with – but about *where*.

Peter's confession doesn't happen in church, turning to the east and looking at the cross or the east window. Let's remember where Caesarea Philippi is: at the heart of the Roman Empire, even named after Caesar and Philip the local governor – and a centre of the worship of Pan. 'The gates of hell' is the name of the neighbouring cave where Pan, the goat-god, was said to be born. Pan was a wild child; wild worship happened there. This was a dark place, in deep thrall to the bondage of human empire and idolatry – not an easy place to confess that Jesus is the Messiah, Son of the living God.

A few years ago I saw the amazing Aztec exhibition at the Guggenheim Museum in New York, and I've always remembered the very last exhibit: the stand that had been used for disembowelling sacrificial victims – and turned by the Jesuits who sought to evangelize the Aztecs into a font. What a sign of courage and confidence in the resurrection. *Where* we proclaim Jesus says a lot about us: Martha proclaims Jesus as the resurrection in the face of the death of Lazarus; Mary Magdalene proclaims the resurrection of Jesus to disciples who have watched his crucifixion; Peter does it in the jaws of the gates of hell. He needs to know the authority of Jesus' words here: 'I will give you the keys of the kingdom of heaven, and whatever you bind on earth will be bound in heaven, and whatever you loose on earth will be loosed in heaven.'

Declaring who is really in charge, which understanding of the world is the true one, is key to binding and loosing in the kingdom of God. It's about performative truth – being able to bring into being what we believe, acting in faith. There's a double naming that goes on, both of false authority ('Get behind me, Satan') and of true spiritual authority. Both Abraham and Peter were given new names, which reflected their God-given identities rather than the failures of their faithless human lives. Understanding our true names means that we become strong enough to allow ourselves to be forgiven and to recover our true purpose and identity. For Peter to know that his true name is 'the rock' means he can recognize his deepest self when Jesus comes to him and gives him a chance to remember his calling after his betrayal.

So let's return to the opening question, 'What sort of a rock is this?' 'Look to the rock from which you were hewn.' It's a beautiful rock, with God's own strength and character, but one that has incorporated into the intricate patterns of its veins the fallibilities of Abraham, who tried to pass his wife off as his sister; the scornful bitter unbelieving laughter of Sarah when the angels told her, in her old age, that she would conceive; and the impulsive ego-driven misunderstanding of Peter. And these are mingled with the strands of the epic faith of Abraham, the perseverance of Sarah and the inclusive leadership of Peter. In its expression as Church it's sometimes rocky soil, a stumbling block rather than a foundation stone, but it's redeemed by finding its identity in the character of God through his Son.

Questions

1 When have you experienced the joy of being wrong as being better than the thrill of being right?
2 'Spiritual authority comes from the whole experience of revelation, forgiveness and faith – and . . . as soon as we try to take our stand on less than the whole of this experience, we seem to enter the territory of human judgement and of loosing our moorings from the gift and promise of God.' Discuss.
3 Binding and loosing – What kinds of binding and loosing do you want to get involved in, and what sorts do you want to avoid?
4 Where are the hardest places you have ever had to witness to your faith?
5 Trust and orthodoxy – What are your reactions to the story of Emperor Constantine? How do you feel about saying the Creed?

6 The Gadarene swine

Luke 8.22–39

One day he got into a boat with his disciples, and he said to them, 'Let us go across to the other side of the lake.' So they put out, and while they were sailing he fell asleep. A gale swept down on the lake, and the boat was filling with water, and they were in danger. They went to him and woke him up, shouting, 'Master, Master, we are perishing!' And he woke up and rebuked the wind and the raging waves; they ceased, and there was a calm. He said to them, 'Where is your faith?' They were afraid and amazed, and said to one another, 'Who then is this, that he commands even the winds and the water, and they obey him?'

Then they arrived at the country of the Gerasenes, which is opposite Galilee. As he stepped out on land, a man of the city who had demons met him. For a long time he had worn no clothes, and he did not live in a house but in the tombs. When he saw Jesus, he fell down before him and shouted at the top of his voice, 'What have you to do with me, Jesus, Son of the Most High God? I beg you, do not torment me' – for Jesus had commanded the unclean spirit to come out of the man. (For many times it had seized him; he was kept under guard and bound with chains and shackles, but he would break the bonds and be driven by the demon into the wilds.) Jesus then asked him, 'What is your name?' He said, 'Legion'; for many demons had entered him. They begged him not to order them to go back into the abyss.

Now there on the hillside a large herd of swine was feeding; and the demons begged Jesus to let them enter these. So he gave them permission. Then the demons came out of the man and entered the swine, and the herd rushed down the steep bank into the lake and was drowned.

When the swineherds saw what had happened, they ran off and told it in the city and in the country. Then people came out to see what had happened, and when they came to Jesus, they found the man from whom the demons had gone sitting at the feet of Jesus, clothed and in his right mind. And they were afraid. Those who had seen it told them how the one who had been possessed by demons had been healed. Then all the people of the surrounding country of the Gerasenes asked Jesus to leave them; for they were seized with great fear. So he got into the boat and returned. The man from whom the demons had gone begged that he might be with him; but Jesus sent him away, saying, 'Return to your home, and declare how much God has done for you.' So he went away, proclaiming throughout the city how much Jesus had done for him.

These two stories appear together, in the same order, in all three of the synoptic Gospels (Matthew 8.28–34; Mark 5.1–20; Luke 8.26–39). The Gospel of John is designed on a different structure completely, and there are not that many episodes in the stories about Jesus' ministry that appear in all three, with two in the same order. So I think it's pretty safe to say that we're talking about the same event here. The basic story is this: Jesus interrupts his mission, gets into a boat at Capernaum to cross the Sea of Galilee, pacifying it on the way. He then destroys a large herd of swine belonging to the Gadarenes (or Gerasenes or Gergasenes) and is asked to depart by the fearful inhabitants. He returns to Capernaum and continues his mission.

The stilling of the storm

The story of the stilling of the storm is very simply told, and practically identical in all three versions. They all carry Jesus' rebuke to his disciples, when he has woken up, of versions of 'Oh you of little faith.' But if you've ever been caught in a storm with seriously big waves, as I once was in a canoe on Loch Lomond as a teenager, you know that it's terrifying.

This story is all about showing Jesus' authority; and having proved it over nature, he turns his attention to the powers and principalities with the exorcism of the demoniac. We might in meditating find it very comforting to know that Jesus will protect us in the storms of life where we venture for his sake, but in the story Jesus is frustrated with his disciples that they haven't already learned to trust the scope of his authority. Perhaps we need to hear a similar message too.

Fear – and fear of death – is very much present in both stories, in a number of ways. 'Help, Lord, we are perishing!' the disciples cry. They really think they're going to die. And the demoniac lives among the tombs – in fact it's as though Legion is entombed – and the very word for this country is that for a wasteland, a pit.

This story, though, presents us with quite a few puzzles. Though translators have tried to even it out in some versions, different places are named in different versions – and this one could be Gadara, Gerasa or Gergasa. Gadara and Gerasa are both inland from the Sea of Galilee, so some have suggested this really happened at Capernaum or somewhere else. There are a few other obvious questions too. What about the swine? Why on earth does Jesus' intervention result in their diving over the cliff into the lake, and why does no one complain? And why aren't the people pleased that this man is restored?

Legion and the legions

Luke tells us that the demonic spirits are named Legion. Why isn't Matthew interested in that detail? I believe it's a very important clue to a highly significant dimension of what's going on here. If we want to find the key connection between these three places and Roman legions, we need to go to Josephus, the historian of *The Jewish War*.[5]

At Capernaum, he describes Jesus of Galilee and his people being pushed back and 6,500 Jews driven into the sea by the legions of Emperor Vespasian. At Gadara, Placidus pursues up to the Jordan and 15,000 perish and 2,200 were captured, including animals. He reports their bloated bodies floating in the Jordan and Dead Sea. Gerasa saw a slaughter too, overseen by Lucius Annius. Wherever the precise location of this miracle, it seems to me that it's got to have a connection with these stories of Roman military might in the shape of the legions slaughtering the Jews in *all* these places.

It puts me in mind of going to the cathedral in Béziers when I was on holiday in the Languedoc a few years ago. It had been the site in 1209 of the massacre of thousands of Cathars – regarded as heretics and brutally slaughtered for their different beliefs. But the Catholics of the town had tried to protect them, and refused to hand them over to the crusaders who came to destroy them – and so were slaughtered with them when they sheltered them in the cathedral. One of the commanders of the crusade, the Abbot of Cîteaux, was reported to have said, 'Kill them all; God knows his own.' Just look what happens when we take right doctrine as the only indicator of faith.

I couldn't go in because it was locked, but as I walked round the side, a shaft of physical pain doubled me up. It was completely isolated – no twinges before or after – and I could only take it as being connected with the slaughter that had happened in that place and the pain that remained there. Slaughter on such a scale leaves a profound impact not just on the people killed and those who love them, but on places for generations. This is a level of structural sin that needs naming as such to begin to heal it in the place and among the communities where it has occurred. I think we can think of plenty of contemporary places where this is still the case.

Why doesn't Matthew make the connection with the Roman slaughters? Perhaps he thinks the 'Legion' connection amounts to making a sick joke at the expense of Jews – perhaps it was still too sensitive to name in Jewish company. Possibly even the Gospel writer can be afraid to name something as huge as this in terms of his people's oppression by the Romans. But isn't it naming and healing this trauma that Jesus is about? Jesus and his Jewish followers were saved from drowning in the sea, and instead of them, the legion of evil spirits are destroyed, and go over the edge into the lake in the bodies of the pigs, just as the Jews had gone over. Isn't this about an exorcism from the trauma inflicted by that oppressive regime, as well as the liberation of individuals caught up in this bad business?

Why pigs – is there some connection here with the fact that the Romans are Gentiles? No one is going to identify pigs with Jews, that's for sure. Why does no one jump up and down about losing 2,000 swine? But would you if that kind of extraordinary point had been made on such a scale? Some see this story as a gateway for mission to the Gentiles, the pork-eaters. This is also a powerful act of naming and non-retaliation – there are no vengeance-killings here.

No wonder the people are struck dumb after the miracle. Perhaps the locals are afraid there will be some imperial retaliation. It's pretty scary when people start challenging the established order, as it had been, I imagine, when Jesus turned the other cheek.[6] Perhaps some are feeling guilty at their collusion with the Romans – maybe they didn't try that hard to defend the Jews who died. This is a kind of fear that often gets in the way of the healing of trauma, the fear that it will be overwhelming and that awful skeletons and collusion and shame might be exposed. But it is the voice of death and fear speaking, the voice of bad binding, not the voice of Jesus and liberation (loosing).

Jesus is demonstrating his authority at the level of removing oppression – and he graphically demonstrates the connection between individual and social oppression. When people are freed from oppression, what often takes the time is living in to the new reality. Helen Bamber,[7] who herself was 20 when she saw people released from concentration camps and who works in the rehabilitation of traumatized asylum seekers, knows how long it takes people to break the patterns of living in fear. Freedom can be frightening.

So whether it is personal or social and structural patterns of behaviour that are changing, some of the healing is about grace to receive the new freedom and to learn new patterns of behaving.

Loosing false names

In the case of Legion, in the case of traumatized refugees, in the case of all of us somewhere along the line, a part of loosing what has bound us is being able to name it for what it is. When you name something, it loses its false authority. This is why the naming of sexual abuse as such is so important. This is why the naming of sin is so important.

Let's turn back to myth and this time to the Brothers Grimm's world of fairy tales. In the story of Rumpelstiltskin[8] a miller has been bragging to the king that his daughter can spin straw into gold. The king puts her to the test, on pain of death. The first night, as she is wondering how on earth she's going to do this, a funny little man comes to her and offers to make it happen if she'll give him something – so she offers him her necklace, he takes the wheel, and spins the straw into gold. The second day the same thing happens, and this time she offers him the ring on her finger. But when the king demands yet more gold to be spun on the third day, and the little man arrives, she has nothing more to give him, so he asks for the promise that she will give him her first child if she marries the king and becomes the queen.

This being a fairy tale, she does indeed become queen and in the fullness of time conceives a child. But she's shocked when the 'manikin' comes back demanding the child that was promised him. Like any mother, she'll do anything to save her child, so pleads with him. He says that if she can discover his name in three days, she can keep the child. So she sends out a messenger, who eventually finds him exulting in his anticipated victory and giving away his name in verse in the process. You really have to read the story to get the full impact, but of course the punchline is that when the miller's daughter discovers his name, and names him to his face, he no longer has the power to hold her baby to ransom. And he self-destructs.

When Jesus names the spirits as 'Legion', and in the process names the guilt and accountability of the Roman legions for the slaughter they have wrought, they no longer have authority to oppress the demoniac, or the region. And the fact that we can't separate out individual healing and release from oppression entirely from the structural issues, demonstrates why healing and exorcism stories are punctuated by calls to witness and action in the world. There is a responsibility to witness to what has happened, not to cover things up again or let the old patterns be repeated or re-established.

Often we feel we're at the mercy of natural conditions, whether it's the weather, our own health or societal circumstances. Jesus asks us to recognize that we're not 'at their mercy'. Faith in his authority can take us to a different place, a place of profound release and a place where we get caught up in a movement of ever more radical change and transformation.

Questions

1 Can you think of places that you feel still bear the marks of traumatic events? What are your own experiences? How are you to understand them?
2 Is it possible to interpret this story without an understanding of sin at a corporate level? How?
3 What parallels can you think of for the Roman oppression of the Jews today? Can you think of a difference a Christian witness has made here?
4 Where have you experienced liberation through naming false authority – or where have you seen it happen?
5 Jesus shows his authority over nature with two signs – what else does this teach us about the nature of his authority?

Week 4
Institutional sin

---

7 The fractal Christ

Colossians 1.15–20

> He is the image of the invisible God, the firstborn of all creation; for in him all things in heaven and on earth were created, things visible and invisible, whether thrones or dominions or rulers or powers – all things have been created through him and for him. He himself is before all things, and in him all things hold together. He is the head of the body, the church; he is the beginning, the firstborn from the dead, so that he might come to have first place in everything. For in him all the fullness of God was pleased to dwell, and through him God was pleased to reconcile to himself all things, whether on earth or in heaven, by making peace through the blood of his cross.

This ancient Christian hymn is one of a matching set. The other one is that beautiful hymn embedded in Philippians that begins:

> Let the same mind be in you that was in Christ Jesus, who, though he was in the form of God, did not regard equality with God as something to be exploited, but emptied himself, taking the form of a slave, being born in human likeness.
>
> (Philippians 2.5–7)

Both have that movement from the pre-existent divinity of Christ – his divine life and work with God before his earthly life – to the humbling reality of human existence and then through to bringing the fullness of his earthly life and death into his resurrected life in and with God. Both were sung in worship in the earliest days of the Church, in very demanding circumstances.

51

Firstborn of creation

This is a huge claim to make, that Jesus Christ can be identified as the firstborn of creation not only with the Word at work with God in the creation of the world – compare Genesis 1 and John 1: 'In the beginning was the Word, and the Word was with God, and the Word was God' – but also with the figure of Wisdom. Wisdom embodies God's presence at work in the world in a way sometimes also identified with the Spirit, especially in the wisdom literature of the Old Testament, and woven through the Gospels.

The Gnostics and Hogwarts

This hymn enters the thought and language world of Colossae (some argue that it may even have been adapted from a pre-existing pagan hymn), where there were some very influential people called Gnostics at the time the letter was written. These people inhabited a tradition with a very sophisticated way of understanding the world, through a complex cosmology of the powers and principalities and authorities who populated it.

It was more exotic and esoteric than the constellation of good and bad wizards and monsters in Harry Potter but, like them, was a way of seeking to get some sort of handle or control on the ways of the world that seemed to be getting completely out of hand. It was a world not really that different from the one we find ourselves in today – perhaps one of the reasons for the runaway success of the Harry Potter books and films. And a bit like one or two of the teachers at Hogwarts, the Gnostics had a tendency to believe that their esoteric knowledge gave them access to a higher magic that meant they didn't have to think in terms of sin or the dependent unknowing of living by faith. And, of course, Harry Potter can teach us a thing or two about the power of naming.

In the Gnostics' world, and in their religion, there was a complicated set of intermediary powers between us and God, and you had to get on the right side of them to win God's favour. They were the spiritual essences of significant powers at work in the world and the bottom line for them was a dualism, a split between good and evil. They had a tendency to think that their understanding of these intermediary powers gave them special access to God and put them above other members of the Christian community.

Powers and principalities

It wasn't only the Gnostics who thought in terms of the powers and principalities. Walter Wink, in his Powers trilogy,[1] makes a very carefully worked argument from an in-depth study of the language of powers and principalities throughout the Bible, to show that it is a major way of understanding the created order. He demonstrates how each of the powers among the systems of the world, be they nations, organizations or churches, has a vocation, a purpose to fulfil in God's economy and kingdom. It is only when the system starts to think it can do it all by itself, without reference to God – does this sound familiar? – that it departs from its highest calling and can become oppressive instead.

Angels

Wink notices how in Revelation, the Spirit addresses the angels of the churches to call them back to their highest purpose. The most famous example is:

> And to the angel of the church in Laodicea write: The words of the Amen, the faithful and true witness, the origin of God's creation:
> 'I know your works; you are neither cold nor hot. I wish that you were either cold or hot. So, because you are lukewarm, and neither cold nor hot, I am about to spit you out of my mouth.'
> (Revelation 3.14–16)

Wink understands these angels as being the corporate personality of the Church, the ethos or spirit or essence that embodies its calling.

But sometimes nations, churches and other powers can operate out of the shadow side of their calling, just as individuals
can. Sometimes, as I know from my work as an organizational
analyst, the shadow of an organization's life is directly related
to the difficulties of the area the organization is working with.
So, for example, if an organization is working with refugees, it
can start to reflect the sense of displacement and trauma of the
people it is serving, which can then undermine its capacity to
operate effectively.

The radical point that Wink is making is the idea that all
human 'systems', in the sense of organizations or powers, have
a spiritual as well as a material dimension, 'things visible and
invisible', rather like individual human beings – and he gives
powerful evidence of it. This is an idea that has been more
or less absent from the modern world, and it makes a huge
difference to the way we think about organizational life – the
way therefore we think about society and work and our global
village – if we take it on board. Sometimes it results in a tendency
only to think about organizations as self-interested, and for
example the capitalist distortion that the ultimate purpose of
a business is its profit rather than what it is offering as a useful
product to the wider context. (Sometimes now we hear about the
triple bottom line for values-driven businesses: people, planet
and profit.) This is in stark contrast to every organization needing to think about its calling in a way that is accountable to
the one who holds all systems together.

Firstborn from the dead

As Christ is named as the one who is 'before all things, and in
him all things hold together', we have to understand that there
is a profound challenge to the Gnostic world of dualism. In
the picture of this hymn, Christ is literally the one in whom
all systems find their place, so there is no question but that
if any of these powers blocks the way to access to God, it has
overstepped the mark, as Christ has opened up this way through

becoming firstborn from the dead. But he has needed to endure the blood of the cross under the oppressive system of the Pax Romana in order to show the greater power of a different, non-violent and loving way. And it is not just the Roman government that has fallen from its highest purpose – there is a terrible tendency for human beings to give all sorts of different systems too much authority and to let them get in the way of our relationship with God, rather than playing their part in the good ordering of God's creation.

So what are the powers and principalities that we hold on to for grim death – instead of holding on to God? Isn't one revealed in the great difficulty we all experience about talking about how we use, how we feel about, money at any depth in our Christian community? Isn't it a bit of a giveaway that there is a set of ideas around money that has become a principality and power setting itself up in opposition to our trust in God and our faith in Christ? The test case is this: can we believe that all things (including money) have been created through him and for him? 'He himself is before all things, and in him all things hold together.' So money, our use of it, our fears and our tight grip of it as the financial systems are rocked, can be brought to Christ who was involved in the creation of the exchange of value that makes the world go round on God's axis.

Image of the invisible God

In the Roman world in which this was written, the 'image of the invisible God' in the form of the emperor's head, imprinted on all the coinage of the empire, was more omnipresent than the Apple logo or the Nike swoosh. Christians died for refusing to worship the image of the emperor. It wasn't that they wanted to cross out 'Emperor' and put 'Jesus' in a like-for-like exchange. If we think of what the Pax Romana involved, with its forcible and brutal policing of the boundaries to retain order within the empire, it is by no means replaced like for like through the peace won by the blood of the cross – in fact this peace is won through direct but non-violent encounter with crucifixion, one of the terrifying enforcers of the 'Roman peace'.

Of course the question arises: aren't there some systems that are irredeemable – that have no higher purpose that their angels can be called back to? What if we think about Nazism, for example? Sometimes it is hard to tell whether a particular organization has ever had a vision of a higher purpose that it can be recalled to. But the issue is that there is a place in the created order for just government, rather than particular regimes, and if the regime can't be called back to that standard, then we need to name it as demonic and resist its authority.

These big claims for Christ as the firstborn of all creation and the firstborn from the dead could easily be seen as grandiose claims to 'big up' another human institution that competes on the same stage, jostling for power with the might of the Roman Empire and the intellectual kudos of the Gnostics. Later on in Christendom we see them used exactly in that way when, for example, Venice steals the Gospel writer Mark's bones from Alexandria to authenticate its political and economic power, or when the struggle to hold the paradox of the image of the invisible God results in the treasures of Europe being poured into reliquaries that then get used as currency for very earthly empire – as anyone who saw the British Museum's 2011 exhibition of relics, 'Treasures of Heaven', will appreciate. Of course, it still goes on, but the Church as Christ's body is still called at its truest to live in the Wisdom of Christ.

Also, I find myself very uneasy about this word 'firstborn'. I'm an eldest child, though of course in our culture it's somewhat mitigated by being female. Birth order plays its part in the struggles of siblings. In fact, looking at how this word is loaded up to include the sense of 'first principle', 'first loved', it makes me realize what a radical story the Prodigal Son is when the younger son is celebrated. All the way through this hymn we are wrestling with hierarchy – as of course the Church and the world continue to wrestle with hierarchy. And yet embedded subversively in this hymn, running like the lettering through a stick of rock, is the idea that Christ is the source in whom all things hold together, and that to win the restoration and reconciliation of all things he has had to leave his lofty position, enter our world and bloody himself on the cross for us.

The fractal Christ

I'd just been wrestling with the principles of organizational design when I was first writing this. My mentor, a man called Aidan, had been trying to get through to me the possibilities of fractal organizations and systems, where every part has the authority of the whole, because the organization is run on principles and functions working to purpose rather than hierarchy. The Bible's insistence on vocation and calling is an insistence about our working to purpose, to God's purpose. So if you were to cut a cross section through any part, in theory, it would have full authority to get on with its life and work, only referring back for issues that are about the co-ordination and calibration of the whole. Easier said than done, of course.

There are many factors that get in the way of our taking up our full authority. But what would it mean for the Church to live up to its calling to be truly fractal – for all of us to be the body of Christ? Wherever you were to cut open the life of the Church – in the home, at work, in the PCC, campaigning – we would see the hallmarks of the presence and authority and self-giving actions of Christ.

And how can we settle for less than believing that God cares for all of our lives, body, mind and spirit, if we really believe in the incarnation? If God loves the whole of created humanity, then what happens in the material world is of as much concern to God as 'spiritual things'. The one affects the other, and in fact they are two poles of the same continuum – both for individuals, organizations and the whole of creation.

At a time when we all feel the increasing bombardment and pressure of daily existence, can we trust Christ to hold all things together even when the shape of our lives seems bashed around? Can we and do we find and claim Christ's peace and power, not some ersatz substitute, amid this storm?

Let's not forget the early liturgies where these words were chanted. People like us, the community of the baptized, brought their lived experience and sought to reorient themselves to their true destiny and identity in Christ. So we have to trust that whatever our life stories may turn out to be, their inconsistencies will be recognized, their sins forgiven and their true meaning revealed if we place ourselves in faith in the hands of the cosmic Christ who makes the invisible God visible to us in all our mess – no special knowledge or access code required.

Questions

1 Who do the Gnostics remind you of in our generation?
2 How possible is it for you to talk about your use of money, both individually and corporately, as a church? What might help talking about it become more normal?
3 What other areas of life have greatest potential to become powers and principalities departing from their true vocation in our culture? How might they be called back?
4 How would you describe the angel or special vocation of your church?
5 How would you describe the angel or vocation of the organization in which you work? (This could include the family system or any club or community to which you belong as well as paid workplaces.)
6 How does a fractal church sound to you?

8 Institutional racism

Romans 11.1–2a, 29–32

I ask, then, has God rejected his people? By no means! I myself
am an Israelite, a descendant of Abraham, a member of the
tribe of Benjamin. God has not rejected his people whom he
foreknew . . . for the gifts and the calling of God are irrevocable.
Just as you were once disobedient to God but have now received
mercy because of their disobedience, so they have now been
disobedient in order that, by the mercy shown to you, they
too may now receive mercy. For God has imprisoned all in
disobedience so that he may be merciful to all.

Matthew 15.10–28

Then he called the crowd to him and said to them, 'Listen and
understand: it is not what goes into the mouth that defiles a
person, but it is what comes out of the mouth that defiles.' Then
the disciples approached and said to him, 'Do you know that
the Pharisees took offence when they heard what you said?' He
answered, 'Every plant that my heavenly Father has not planted
will be uprooted. Let them alone; they are blind guides of the
blind. And if one blind person guides another, both will fall
into a pit.' But Peter said to him, 'Explain this parable to us.'
Then he said, 'Are you also still without understanding? Do you
not see that whatever goes into the mouth enters the stomach,
and goes out into the sewer? But what comes out of the mouth
proceeds from the heart, and this is what defiles. For out of the
heart come evil intentions, murder, adultery, fornication, theft,
false witness, slander. These are what defile a person, but to eat
with unwashed hands does not defile.'

Jesus left that place and went away to the district of Tyre and
Sidon. Just then a Canaanite woman from that region came out
and started shouting, 'Have mercy on me, Lord, Son of David;
my daughter is tormented by a demon.' But he did not answer
her at all. And his disciples came and urged him, saying, 'Send
her away, for she keeps shouting after us.' He answered, 'I was
sent only to the lost sheep of the house of Israel.' But she came

and knelt before him, saying, 'Lord, help me.' He answered, 'It is not fair to take the children's food and throw it to the dogs.' She said, 'Yes, Lord, yet even the dogs eat the crumbs that fall from their masters' table.' Then Jesus answered her, 'Woman, great is your faith! Let it be done for you as you wish.' And her daughter was healed instantly.

It was a shock to me, as I heaved the rucksack off my shoulders and wandered into the little café to get a beer, on day eight of my serene pastoral pilgrimage in 2011 on the *Chemin* (the French part of the pilgrim route to Santiago de Compostela), to find the front page of the newspaper *Midi Libre* full of the riots in England; and the next day to be confronted – on the front page of *Le Monde* – with images of burnt-out cars on Clarence Road, just down from where I live in Hackney in east London. Inside, in a double-page spread, was a picture of the Rector of Hackney out on the streets trying to calm things down. It was in this context that I revisited a passage that was already a major touchstone for me in terms of understanding institutional sin.

For me the story of the Syro-Phoenician woman – as Mark calls it in his version – was one that radicalized my view of Jesus at another time of national tension: the Stephen Lawrence Inquiry. It was then that it first really hit me that Jesus, in this story, finds himself caught up in a web of what the then Bishop of Stepney, John Sentamu, and others on the Stephen Lawrence Inquiry (chaired by Sir William Macpherson), defined as 'institutional racism' – in other words, racism that somehow the system manages to collude in and fails to challenge. In the Stephen Lawrence case it was the Metropolitan Police who failed to prosecute those who killed Stephen Lawrence in 1993. It was only in 2012 – nearly 18 years after his death – that two men were finally convicted of racially motivated murder, after the cold case had been reopened by the acting deputy commissioner, Cressida Dick.

In the case of Jesus, he belonged to a religious institution – Judaism – and an ethnic community that somehow were failing to recognize the full humanity of a woman from beyond both the institution and the ethnic group. His direct interaction with the woman, however, could not have gone more differently from that of the gang of youths who encountered Stephen Lawrence that night in 1993.

John Sentamu was then my bishop in the Stepney area of London Diocese and is the Archbishop of York at the time of writing. He is the only bishop to have been stopped and searched eight times in the UK, to my knowledge at least. As well as being a black man, he is an advocate of the High Court of Uganda. In the time of Amin, among other things he defended the rights of the Ugandan Asians who were being discriminated against, so he was an obvious choice for the Stephen Lawrence Inquiry.

Dogs and puppies

In this encounter, Jesus calls the woman a 'dog' (there's no getting around it by translating it as 'puppy', as some have tried to do), a standard term in his culture for these non-Jewish pagans who, Matthew reminds us (by using the term Canaanite instead of Syro-Phoenician), have been enemies of Israel since the time of Noah. I suppose it's a bit like referring to a Muslim as a Saracen, evoking the crusades. The thing that forced me to wrestle with it was my own understanding of what it meant for Jesus to be fully human, and how that affected what it meant for him to be without sin.

Isn't it the point of 'institutional racism' that it's part of our institutional and therefore cultural assumptions, so we can't see it for what it is – the air we breathe – until some incident brings it out into the open? It isn't deliberate until something happens that challenges us to see it for what it is, and question our collusion with it. At that point we start to have responsibility for whether we collude or challenge.

Here is a story that challenges Jesus about how to interpret his calling and to see what is a distraction from it. He doesn't answer the woman when she approaches him, even though she uses the terms to address him that show that she's been listening, that she believes he has real authority that she accepts on Jewish terms: 'Have mercy on me, Lord, Son of David.' He doesn't answer her because, in his society, to answer a woman who addressed you in a public place would be to recognize her call upon you, and as he says to the watching disciples, 'I was sent only to the lost sheep of the house of Israel.' Up to now that means to have nothing to do with Gentiles. But he stops short of sending her away as they urge him to.

Here is a story that shows us what it means to have great faith. After the first rebuff she kneels before him, again calling, 'Lord, help me.' Now he feels the need to justify his position to her. He has to be fair to the children of Israel. He must give them their due inheritance. 'Yes, Lord, but even the dogs eat what drops from the master's table.' She doesn't challenge any of his categories. She asks for mercy and continues to believe in his power to meet her need. She completely disarms him and he recognizes in her cry the voice of faith, of great faith.

How to lose and win an argument at the same time

Here's a story where Jesus appears to lose the argument while in fact being persuaded by the full logic of the compelling argument he's just won with the Pharisees. This argument was about how you really discern what's clean and what's unclean, who's to be included and who excluded.

He hears her cry. She turns his argument from one of right to one of grace. 'Even the dogs gather up the crumbs from under thy table.' Cranmer understood about this approach and left it to us as one of the treasures of the BCP Communion Service that echoes her words in making us the ones who 'are not worthy so much as to gather up the crumbs under thy table' and bringing us to 'the same Lord, whose property is always to have mercy'. And while I think that sometimes he's in danger of keeping us here (in a position of not being worthy), Cranmer has grasped something about the heart of faith from this story. And perhaps this is what enabled him to write a liturgy that was able to bridge the terrible divide between Protestant and Catholic, which resulted in many more deaths than the 2011 summer riots in the hideous burnings at the stake that happened all over the country within view of the great cathedrals. Faith does not stand upon its rights but throws itself upon God's mercy.

The voices of Wisdom

When Jesus is confronted by this cry, he cannot stand on the terms of his calling – it calls forth the compassion within his heart. This is after all where he encounters the source of his calling in God's love, whereas his understanding up to that moment of its terms and conditions has been through the shared current institutional and cultural understandings of what it means to be a good Jew – which has lost touch with the crucial idea that 'it is not the children of the [Abraham's] flesh who are the children of God, but the children of the promise are counted as descendants' (Romans 9.8). In Luke's Gospel Jesus claims to be Wisdom. One of the hallmarks of Wisdom is to listen to the cries of the poor – the poor in spirit, the poor economically, the outsiders, the excluded ones. The same word, a word that conjures up shrieking with desperation, is used for this woman's cry as is used for Peter's cry to Jesus as he starts to sink in the sea when he tries to walk on the water.

How are followers of Jesus, given the spirit of Wisdom, to respond to the cries on the street? What about the cry of Tariq Jahan, who lost his son as he sought to defend property from rioters in Birmingham in August 2011 – a cry for peace and a cry of belonging from a Muslim, one who had just had his son ripped away from him? What about the cries of his community and the leaders who urged other Muslims not to retaliate; the cries of Ramallah, of Bethlehem, the Wailing Wall, the Lebanon and Tahrir Square?

Which are the unexpected voices when we hear, as with the Canaanite woman, the voice of faith? It may not have the ritual trappings of faith. It may not come with a shared idea of what constitutes propriety and beautifully ordered worship in church. Where do we hear the voices that demonstrate, from what they utter, that they are not defiled but responsive to the word of God?

This is a time when all of us are called to listen with the spirit of Wisdom to the cries of our time; to be open, like Jesus, to being challenged as to how we are going to be called to be true to the deepest part of our faith, and how that might change and subvert some of our most dearly held assumptions about it.

Inclusion and exclusion

We've heard something about the inclusion of Muslims. What about the Romans passage and the inclusion of the Jews? This is something I saw the relevance of afresh when I met a handsome young Frenchman on my pilgrimage. He claimed to be simply out for a walk – it was also a long-distance footpath – but he turned out to have been reading the Gospel on the quiet, and wanted, under cover of darkness like Nicodemus, on a walk under the stars on the Aubrac plateau, to know what Christianity had to say about the Jewish people. Not so surprising, really, given that he had one Jewish parent and one Christian one.

At the end of the great argument for mission to the Gentiles, in Romans, from Paul, the Pharisee of Pharisees, comes his return to the question of the Jewish people, the chosen ones, the vine into which the Gentiles have been grafted. Paul asks the question: 'Now if their stumbling means riches for the world, and if their defeat means riches for Gentiles, how much more will their full inclusion mean!' (Romans 11.12). The last word with God, again, is not judgement but grace and mercy. Human hardness of heart is turned in God's sovereignty to the reconciliation of the world.

This is not just a New Testament message. Look no further than Isaiah 56 to see how far in the Jewish story of God the idea of the inclusion of the Gentiles and of all the peoples of the world had come into their self-understanding as God's chosen people: 'My house shall be called a house of prayer for all peoples. Thus says the Lord GOD, who gathers the outcasts of Israel, I will gather others to them besides those already gathered' (Isaiah 56.7b–8).

But where does this theme of the inclusion of the Jews fit into the story as it reaches us today? I felt I could not ignore it in the light of those two encounters – Jesus' highlighting the saving of the Jews after their persecution in the exorcism of Legion, and his broadening of his understanding of his mission to the Gentiles in the incident with the Canaanite woman. It certainly calls us back to the need for an ongoing dialogue and conversation with our Jewish brothers and sisters – something we can easily think of as an optional extra. Does it not take us back to the Pharisees, the total insiders in terms of the law? Might we not think of them as the people most sure of their own inclusion, whether it's the bankers in terms of the economy, the products of the oldest public schools ruling the country, or even ourselves?

Though Jesus speaks a message of judgement to the legalism of the Pharisees, for using the law to create barriers of exclusion, it is not in the service of creating another barrier of exclusion for them. It is rather to call them back to the authentic vision of God's ministry of reconciliation right from the start, which they had had the best chance to understand and to serve. He binds their binding and looses their loosing. So it's no use our seeking, in the service of retrieving the excluded in our society, to create another set of excluded and outcast, another set of scapegoats and outsiders. Apart from losing the enormous potential of their full transformed contribution to society, that would be missing the point of the God who always seeks out the lost, whether they are the lost sheep of Israel or simply the one that has strayed from the ninety-nine; who always seeks to reincorporate us into one body through his Son.

Questions

1 How do you find the idea that Jesus, by virtue of being fully human, might be caught up in a web of institutional sin, and that we, like him, have to find ways to challenge it and ourselves when it surfaces, from our deepest place of calling and compassion?

2 What are the areas of institutional sin we find ourselves noticing and being challenged by?

3 Who are the people we might need to reconsider in our own categories of clean and unclean in the church? Are we prepared to lose one argument in the interests of being converted by a deeper principle?

4 Where has Wisdom brought to your attention voices that need to be heard recently?

5 Who are we most tempted to exclude in our desire to include others? What does it mean to keep on including them too?

Week 5
Darkness into light

---

9 Dazzling darkness

Acts 9.1–20

Meanwhile Saul, still breathing threats and murder against the disciples of the Lord, went to the high priest and asked him for letters to the synagogues at Damascus, so that if he found any who belonged to the Way, men or women, he might bring them bound to Jerusalem. Now as he was going along and approaching Damascus, suddenly a light from heaven flashed around him. He fell to the ground and heard a voice saying to him, 'Saul, Saul, why do you persecute me?' He asked, 'Who are you, Lord?' The reply came, 'I am Jesus, whom you are persecuting. But get up and enter the city, and you will be told what you are to do.' The men who were travelling with him stood speechless because they heard the voice but saw no one. Saul got up from the ground, and though his eyes were open, he could see nothing; so they led him by the hand and brought him into Damascus. For three days he was without sight, and neither ate nor drank.

Now there was a disciple in Damascus named Ananias. The Lord said to him in a vision, 'Ananias.' He answered, 'Here I am, Lord.' The Lord said to him, 'Get up and go to the street called Straight, and at the house of Judas look for a man of Tarsus named Saul. At this moment he is praying, and he has seen in a vision a man named Ananias come in and lay his hands on him so that he might regain his sight.' But Ananias answered, 'Lord, I have heard from many about this man, how much evil he has done to your saints in Jerusalem; and here he has authority from the chief priests to bind all who invoke your name.' But the Lord said to him, 'Go, for he is an instrument whom I have chosen to bring my name before Gentiles and

67

kings and before the people of Israel; I myself will show him how much he must suffer for the sake of my name.' So Ananias went and entered the house. He laid his hands on Saul and said, 'Brother Saul, the Lord Jesus, who appeared to you on your way here, has sent me so that you may regain your sight and be filled with the Holy Spirit.' And immediately something like scales fell from his eyes, and his sight was restored. Then he got up and was baptized, and after taking some food, he regained his strength.

For several days he was with the disciples in Damascus, and immediately he began to proclaim Jesus in the synagogues, saying, 'He is the Son of God.'

So here, if we needed it, is the evidence that Jesus was not out to create another set of excluded scapegoats through his challenging of the scribes and Pharisees. Paul's is the classic conversion story of the insider from Jewish faith, a man who persecuted Christians in his zeal for the law but was the one God chose to be the apostle of apostles to the Gentiles, and who would come to understand it theologically in terms of fulfilling the vocation of Israel. One of the most wonderful things about conversion and calling – I'm going to argue, on the basis of this story, that the two are inseparable – is that each of us is called to be most fully the person God has created us to be. Of course, that person doesn't look like anyone else and indeed, in its fullest expression, might appear unrecognizable from what we could have imagined – and yet on closer examination be the mature expression of the same DNA. So, fundamentally, when light is shone on our darkness, our sin, we find a portal to help us discover our true purpose.

Saul of Tarsus

In Saul we have a Jewish man, very well versed in his faith, taught in the Oxford and Cambridge of Jewish seminaries, 'zealous for the law' in biblical phraseology. He hates the idea of Jesus of Nazareth, so much so that he's voted for the death of Christians, locked them up in prisons and is now pursuing them violently even on foreign soil. And he's well in with the chief priests – enough to have their blessing for his project. So, unlike a lot of converts, he already has a relationship with Jesus, but it's as persecutor, as Jesus himself tells him.

The Torah terrorist

When Saul came to faith he was a man of the law – not of the state secular law, though he knew how to claim his rights as a Roman citizen, but as a Jewish religious leader versed in the Torah, the law of God. He was a fundamentalist Sharia man if you like (though we could just as accurately say a fundamentalist Levitical man), someone for whom the imperative of religious law applied to everyone, not just those who were fellow believers. He went around applying it with a violence not unlike some of our worst associations with fundamentalism – persecuting Christians because of their different attitude to his tradition, to the extent of being directly involved in the stoning of Stephen, the first Christian martyr.

Let me unpack my throwaway comments about Sharia and Levitical law – they are important for helping us understand how we too struggle with some of the things with which Saul was wrestling. As Rowan Williams pointed out, to widespread derision at the time because people couldn't hear what he was saying, Sharia law is one expression of a kind of religious law that needs to be incorporated into civil legal structures to make it work for that community. He reminded us that we'd made that sort of accommodation for a long time in British law by making special provision for Jewish people in the area of marriage law. This provision is only for them and doesn't affect anyone else's rights or freedoms.

This is in the context of needing to recognize that British law has its deepest roots in principles from the Christian tradition, and that we are now working out what it means to live in a society with people from many different faith traditions. St Paul's

Cross, for example, in the churchyard of St Paul's Cathedral, was the gathering point for a 'folkmoot', or general assembly, of the people called by the King's Justice in 1236 to announce that Henry III wished London to be well governed and have its liberties guarded. The Archbishop of Canterbury and the king attended the meeting there in 1259 when Londoners came to swear allegiance to the king and his heirs (admittedly under duress, as a royal army was holding the city gates at the time).

So our present archbishop was foreseeing that before too long we would need to accommodate, for example, ways for Muslims to get mortgages that didn't transgress Islam's prohibitions against usury. Again, it doesn't impinge on anyone else's freedom – and in fact might have something prophetic to say to the debt a lot of us bind ourselves up in through mortgages. But the outraged, incandescent reaction from large swathes of the media and society in general came because their associations of the word 'Sharia' were with ideas that led to terrorism and 9/11 in particular – ideas where a particular view of Islamic law led some Muslims into violent acts against any people, of whatever religious background, who didn't agree with them. You could say that Saul of Tarsus, despite his pedigree education, had crossed that line with the persecution of Stephen. He had become a Torah terrorist.

Being unhorsed

We will all have our own mental images of what it looks like when Saul is blinded by the light of his encounter with Jesus. There's nothing in the passage that confirms Saul was riding a horse, but there are things about Caravaggio's two famous portrayals of this moment that I find very truthful to the feeling of what is happening, even if not to the fact.

I'd like to use these two paintings to help us think about Saul. The first shows us his armoured supporter vainly attempting to defend him with a spear and shield from the non-violent crucified love of Jesus. As Martin Warner says:

> Their armour is no use against this love . . . Paul, by contrast,
> is stripped of his defences, the external loss of his armour being
> a symbol of his internal, spiritual exposure to the irresistible
> grace of God that he was seeking in his own way.[1]

Saul's body language shrieks exposure: here is a gentle, reconciling love that he cannot resist.

In Caravaggio's second depiction of the scene, the horse becomes far more prominent. Neither horse nor groom can see the light. Saul is completely undone. The light that in the first painting we can see illuminating certain things – dislocating them from everyday experience – is now completely overwhelming him. Everything is different now. There is no visible Jesus in this version, but the power of God is revealed as the light invading, overcoming the darkness.

We don't need the paintings to know that even if he wasn't wearing physical armour, Saul had been defending himself with metaphorical armour, which was now completely useless in the face of this disruption of grace. Both paintings point to the decentring of self or ego, of thinking we're in control of our own destiny. The horse is often used as an image of the human psyche in the world of the unconscious: we might think of ourselves as controlling our lives; the picture of coming off a horse reminds us we're both horse and rider. And Jesus has to do something dramatic to put Saul in touch with his more instinctual self – a bit like the experience of Chiron the centaur we thought about on page 16.

Blinded by the light: dazzling darkness

Trying to resist the love of the crucified one with armour doesn't work. The experience of being brought to a halt, unhorsed, stopped in our tracks through some sort of crisis, is sometimes what we need if we refuse to face the splits in the way we see the world. This can be both about the parts of ourselves that we're unable to bring into view and so can't integrate with the parts we're more comfortable with, and about our experiences of when we start to see that the way we're living our lives just isn't working any more.

It can't have been very comfortable being Saul the Pharisee. In my experience, those who feel the need to persecute others are often just as persecutory towards themselves. And it's only when we relinquish that internal violence that we can stop inflicting it on others.

God wasn't 'done' with Saul once he first saw the light. Converted, he remained stubborn and blind. Converted, we remain stubborn and blind. He needed, and we too need, time – time when we're slowed down or somehow derailed so that we have space enough to confront these splits, to hear and see truly.

Resisting newness

'See, I make all things new!' These are the words of the risen Christ from the vision of Revelation. Yet how strongly we resist this newness, how often we cling to our 'systems of death'. This is an area of thinking that's been well explored by Marcus Borg,[2] Walter Wink[3] and Walter Brueggemann[4] in their writings. For example, the law becomes a system of death when it exists to set up the persecuting of difference – as with Saul's persecution of Christians and Jesus' crucifixion under the system of death that went under the name of Pax Romana.

Systems of death exist in the world and in our internal worlds – patterns of thought and behaviour that persecute the possibility of our participating in the authenticity and newness that the risen Christ will offer us. Such an experience is actually one of healing and integration, of being brought in touch more with who we truly are. And yet it's often experienced as and characterized by a sense of discontinuity and disruption – of being brought to a halt.

Even Paul the activist is taken by the spirit into quiet seclusion, very uncharacteristically, as there is a lot of inner work to be done. But he is someone who already understands from his Saul days the notion of calling – at least he doesn't have the split that causes many of us in our age to separate belief and how we prioritize the ways we spend our lives. Before he was prepared to make crusading journeys to persecute Christians; now he will give himself totally to reaching out to the Gentiles. The most Jewish Jew is to become the evangelist of the Gentiles, the very group of people he found it most difficult to accept among the followers of Jesus because they hadn't been brought up in the way of the law.

The integrity of vocation – paradigm shifts included

As Marcus Borg and John Dominic Crossan have observed,[5] Saul's conversion didn't do violence to his deepest identity but opened up another, unimagined, way of being a faithful Jew, from Pharisaic Jew to Christian Jew – with a mystical experience. His fears of Jesus would undoubtedly have included the fear of betraying his God-given calling. But conversion of life is not about making us who we're not but more truly who we are. It's just that it can sometimes look radically different from what we might have dreamed.

Paul has to learn, through his direct encounter with the risen Lord, very new things. The first is to open up the possibility of seeing Christ and therefore God in all people. Jesus told him that when he was persecuting Christians he was persecuting him. When we persecute or demean anyone, it is Christ we are mistreating. This fiercely proud man also has to learn to be dependent on another. In Saul's case it is Ananias, who though very different has to go through his own more gradual process of call and conversion to learn to see his persecutor, Saul, as Paul, his brother.

The life of conversion means we have to keep being open to such shifts in the way we see the world, with the compass and rudder of coming to understand how these shifts are actually true north to our fundamental calling and identity. How else would the Church ever have got involved in the abolition of slavery, the emancipation of women or the green movement?

Again we see how individual conversion and corporate conversion go hand in hand and how sometimes the dazzling light needs to come through blinding darkness[6] to defuse our attachment to systems of death.

Questions

1 How might our cultural bias, our other givens, assumptions and certainties, blind us, causing us to 'breathe threats and destruction' where God might be calling us to enlarge our vision?
2 Can you identify with the experience of being 'unhorsed'? How?
3 What are the systems of death we live under?
4 What examples can you give from your own life of how you've ended up making a paradigm shift that took you into a place you never thought possible? Did it reconnect you with a deep sense of vocation?
5 What are the telltale signs of resisting newness?

10 A life-and-death struggle

Romans 8.6–11

> To set the mind on the flesh is death, but to set the mind on the Spirit is life and peace. For this reason the mind that is set on the flesh is hostile to God; it does not submit to God's law – indeed it cannot, and those who are in the flesh cannot please God.
>
> But you are not in the flesh; you are in the Spirit, since the Spirit of God dwells in you. Anyone who does not have the Spirit of Christ does not belong to him. But if Christ is in you, though the body is dead because of sin, the Spirit is life because of righteousness. If the Spirit of him who raised Jesus from the dead dwells in you, he who raised Christ from the dead will give life to your mortal bodies also through his Spirit that dwells in you.

Decluttering

My theme for Lent in 2008 was that of decluttering. I'd needed to engage with it because I'd just downsized from a five-bedroom bungalow via a one-bedroom flat to a more permanent two-bedroom flat – and finally now needed to deal with a lot of things still in store. This process of decluttering, creating a new space in which to live, led me to see that I was also going through a process of working out what to hold on to. I felt that this was an internal as well as an external process. A lot of my things had associations with different parts of my life and therefore challenged me to see, amid the joys and the struggles they put me in touch with, that this process has a spiritual dimension to which it might be important to pay attention.

I'd made some mistakes: I found that in my anxiety to clear the space, my impatience to be freed from the clutter, I'd rashly got rid of some things I then realized would have been very useful – because I couldn't see where they'd go or didn't see them as mine or belonging to my life, such as some of the things I'd inherited in the new flat. I found people who were willing to help me store some things for a while, and began to realize what a ministry that is, both literally and metaphorically. People who are patient with us while we sort through our clutter, whether physical, mental, emotional or spiritual, are to be treasured.

I tried to understand that the way I disposed of the things I no longer needed had significance too – recycling where possible, working out to whom I could give things or return things. I had a hilarious moment with a chair, finding myself sitting on it on the street singing 'Happy Birthday' to my friend before giving it to her. I discovered that the disciplines of giving things away and returning things helped me reconnect with people.

There were big frustrations: finding it all too difficult and fleeing the task, then realizing afterwards that I absolutely couldn't cope without a more ordered home and base; tripping over all the stuff I hadn't yet sorted through; having a visit from my mum and finding I still had too much clutter to find ways of letting her help and letting her be.

This flat, the first I had owned (or rather had a big mortgage on), which was to have been the symbol of being grown up, started to raise questions for me about whether anything had changed in my life at all, or whether I was still struggling with all the same things as before. Had I got rid of any of my baggage?

I wonder what kind of connections you find yourself making with this story and with your own journey this Lent, as well as with your own experience of the stickiness of patterns of sin. It is to this kind of experience that Paul speaks in this section of his extraordinary letter to the Romans.

Sometimes Paul's writing can feel very dense, very abstract, and yet it's full of his experience, what's actually happened to him. We've already thought about that blinding light on the Damascus Road, his encounter with Christ and the challenge to move from persecuting Christ to completely reframing his understanding of his calling, to become the apostle to the Gentiles. Then there was his time in seclusion, to be sorted out and decluttered by God in privacy, followed by his return to the spotlight of apostolic leadership and the exposure of his shortcomings as well as his strengths. Just think about the fallings-out he had with his colleagues – such as the very public one with Barnabas in Acts 15 over whether or not John Mark should come along with them. Not an easy person to work with, Paul.

Doing what we don't want to do

So I want us to try to apprehend what Paul is saying in a way that we can connect with our own experience. He speaks in chapter 7 of Romans about the extreme frustration of knowing that he wants to live a different way in the light of his relationship with God through Christ, but consistently finding himself repeating his old patterns: 'I do not do what I want, but I do the very thing I hate' (7.15).

People who are very harsh with others are often so because they're very harsh with themselves, so how do they develop the capacity to behave any differently? In his encounter with the risen Christ, Paul realizes that he is freed from this constant pressure to conform to the letter of the law in the knowledge that he just can't do it; he can give up the hopeless attempt to maintain his persona of being a righteous person, a respectable, good person, by his own efforts.

When he meets with Jesus, when Jesus' followers teach him the way of Christ, he's flooded with the freedom of being forgiven, with the knowledge that he's loved by God just as he is, with all of his faults, and that this holy and loving God is calling him to follow him. Because he is being loved, he begins to drop his guard; he starts to dare to face up to who he really is, some of the dark attitudes that lurk under those robes of respectability and judgement. But as he does so, his experience is that though he knows this wonderful love of God, there are still deep-rooted patterns of behaviour in his life that he feels powerless to change: 'Wretched man that I am! Who will rescue me from this body of death?' (7.24). He knows the love of God, but his pattern is still to judge and condemn both himself and others. He hasn't got rid of lots of the old furniture yet, nor chucked out the toxic letters. 'So then, with my mind I am a slave to the law of God, but with my flesh I am a slave to the law of sin' (7.25b).

But when we meet him in this passage, Paul has fastened himself to the greater reality: 'There is therefore now no condemnation for those who are in Christ Jesus. For the law of the Spirit of life in Christ Jesus has set you free from the law of sin and of death' (Romans 8.1–2).

God has fulfilled the demands of the law through Jesus, so that we do not have to stand under its condemnation after all. It is the work of the coming weeks to wrestle afresh with what that meant – with how Jesus dealt with our sin and to find afresh the forgiving love that is stronger than sin and death. And it is our work today to gain a foretaste of the life and freedom that that love has won for us.

It might seem odd to use the word 'work' when this passage is all about the grace that lifts us beyond the law and beyond the scope of anything we can do for ourselves to lift ourselves out of clutter and baggage and deeply ingrained habits of life lived in independence of God, failing to apprehend his love. This is no work of our own, but it is the grace of God in the life of Christ, expressed through the gift of the Spirit to us, something we can respond to actively with all this spiritual energy working so mightily within us.

What does this mean, 'To set the mind on the flesh is death, but to set the mind on the Spirit is life and peace'? Well, let's kick off with what it doesn't mean. It doesn't mean that anything to do with our physical bodies, and especially to do with sex, is automatically suspect or bad. Nor does it mean that our humanity is automatically bad. Jesus after all took on the fullness of human nature, as the Chalcedonian Creed puts it, 'like unto us, [yet] without sin'.

To live according to *sarx*, the word here for flesh, means to live in a way that is a distortion of our true selves. We're made in the image and likeness of God, we're designed for relationship with him, so when we live focusing on ourselves, forgetting God and the rest of the world to which we're connected, that's a distortion of our true selves. So when we treat our bodies as though they were just for ourselves, in the way we eat or behave sexually, yes, that is sinful, but perhaps no more so than when we use our minds or imaginations in the same way, as though we lived just for ourselves and without reference to God, which leads us into other kinds of embodied action that are destructive to others and ourselves.

Heart-work is hard work

To 'set the mind on the Spirit', on the other hand, involves a fundamental shift in identity. As one of the seventeenth-century Puritans, John Flavel, says in his classic work, *Keeping the Heart*, 'The greatest difficulty in conversion, is to win the heart to God; and the greatest difficulty after conversion, is to keep the heart with God . . . It is the *hardest* work: heart-work is hard work indeed.'[7] So what does this kind of 'heart-work' look like?

- It looks like stopping the vain attempt to improve ourselves.
- It looks like accepting ourselves, with all our human frailty and weakness – something we can only do if we can first accept God's grace.
- It looks like opening ourselves up to being loved, which we can only do by dropping our defences and pretences.
- It looks like accepting God's love and stopping fighting.

Love sees us as we are and loves us anyway. But love does not settle for the status quo where that is ruining the loved one's life.

> But if Christ is in you, though the body is dead because of sin, the Spirit is life because of righteousness. If the Spirit of him

who raised Jesus from the dead dwells in you, he who raised Christ from the dead will give life to your mortal bodies also through his Spirit that dwells in you. (8.10–11)

Paul hasn't lost sight of the struggle we endure in between discovering the newness and freedom of the love of God and feeling dragged down by our old patterns. But he knows that life – the resurrection life won for us by Jesus – is stronger than death. The old ways can never ultimately defeat us; our situation can never be impossible for God, too difficult for God to redeem and transform.

The lectionary writers pair this passage of St Paul with the story of the raising of Lazarus in John 11.1–45. Jesus demonstrates through this act that his life is stronger than death. When we are confronted with physical death we are met with all the outrageous consequences of life under the law of sin and death: the distress, the disorientation, the disarray in our relationships with family and friends, the disgust we attach to the stink of a human corpse or the disengagement of the stiffness of an embalmed body. God is our creator: the consequence of life lived apart from him is death.

Getting over death

Jesus raises Lazarus, and on his own timescale. He weeps for his loss. He is a human embodied, emotional being. He is beside himself with anger at the separation of death. He needs his friends and followers to realize that his purpose is to bring life beyond death. He calls Lazarus out of the tomb when he is well and truly dead – when 'he stinketh', as the King James Version graphically puts it. He calls him to 'come out' as he will later call the fearful infant Church to come out from its locked room, to live a resurrection life that is no longer afraid of sin or death.

Lazarus will die again, when his time is come, and Jesus has to go on to the place of his own death. Jesus wants to free us from everything that stops us apprehending that:

80

neither death, nor life, nor angels, nor rulers, nor things present, nor things to come, nor powers, nor height, nor depth, nor anything else in all creation, will be able to separate us from the love of God in Christ Jesus our Lord.   (Romans 8.38–39)

'Thanks be to God, who gives us the victory through our Lord Jesus Christ' (1 Corinthians 15.57).

Questions

1 Decluttering – how do you connect with the notion of decluttering at different levels?
2 How do you recognize the experience of doing what you don't want to do?
3 'Heart-work is hard work.' Discuss. You may find John Flavel's *Keeping the Heart* a useful resource. It is readily available online (see endnotes).
4 What does it mean for death not to be the last word?

Week 6
Seeing in the dark

———— •◆•• ————

11 Opening to the light

Isaiah 61.1–11

The spirit of the Lord GOD is upon me, because the LORD has anointed me; he has sent me to bring good news to the oppressed, to bind up the broken-hearted, to proclaim liberty to the captives, and release to the prisoners; to proclaim the year of the LORD's favour, and the day of vengeance of our God; to comfort all who mourn; to provide for those who mourn in Zion – to give them a garland instead of ashes, the oil of gladness instead of mourning, the mantle of praise instead of a faint spirit. They will be called oaks of righteousness, the planting of the LORD, to display his glory. They shall build up the ancient ruins, they shall raise up the former devastations; they shall repair the ruined cities, the devastations of many generations.

Strangers shall stand and feed your flocks, foreigners shall till your land and dress your vines; but you shall be called priests of the LORD, you shall be named ministers of our God; you shall enjoy the wealth of the nations, and in their riches you shall glory. Because their shame was double, and dishonour was proclaimed as their lot, therefore they shall possess a double portion; everlasting joy shall be theirs.

For I the LORD love justice, I hate robbery and wrongdoing; I will faithfully give them their recompense, and I will make an everlasting covenant with them. Their descendants shall be known among the nations, and their offspring among the peoples; all who see them shall acknowledge that they are a people whom the LORD has blessed. I will greatly rejoice in the LORD, my whole being shall exult in my God; for he has clothed me with the garments of salvation, he has covered me with the robe of righteousness, as a bridegroom decks himself with a garland, and as a bride adorns herself with her jewels. For as the earth brings forth its shoots, and as a garden causes what is sown in it to spring up, so the Lord GOD will cause righteousness and praise to spring up before all the nations.

John 1.6–14

There was a man sent from God, whose name was John. He came as a witness to testify to the light, so that all might believe through him. He himself was not the light, but he came to testify to the light. The true light, which enlightens everyone, was coming into the world.

He was in the world, and the world came into being through him; yet the world did not know him. He came to what was his own, and his own people did not accept him. But to all who received him, who believed in his name, he gave power to become children of God, who were born, not of blood or of the will of the flesh or of the will of man, but of God.

And the Word became flesh and lived among us, and we have seen his glory, the glory as of a father's only son, full of grace and truth.

My eye was taken by a piece of graffiti photographed and shared on Facebook recently. It said, 'Due to recent budget cuts, the light at the end of the tunnel has just been switched off.'

Newgrange

In 3200 BC, a workforce of 300 spent 20 years constructing a tomb. It was no ordinary tomb, but the passage tomb at Newgrange in Ireland – a huge mound marked by standing stones, obscure and mystical Celtic swirls. The long passage or tunnel of 19 metres leads to a burial chamber deep within, which resides in total darkness except for dawn on the winter solstice (21 December and a few mornings after), when for 17 minutes the sun is at a low enough angle to make its way all the way along the passage to bring light into the dark centre of the tomb chamber. Even after standing in the darkness for just a few minutes, the return of the light is enough to make the hairs on the back of your neck stand on end.

Until there is a glimmer of light our eyes are helpless – they cannot even begin to acclimatize to the darkness. Once there is the tiniest crack of light, our eyes set to work and begin to adapt, to make out the forms, even though it may take them some time. They are remarkably sensitive, and their design assumes the existence of light.

John the Baptist, according to the Gospel of John, was a witness to the light – the spiritual light. He knew he wasn't the light himself but when he recognized that a shaft of light had entered his world, he kept his eyes focused on it and encouraged everyone he could to do the same. The point of the baptism of repentance was to prepare eyes for the light. John, in his description, does not even mention John's baptism until the end: he thinks in terms of John's relationship to the light.

A decentred life

John defined himself entirely by what he was not – he decentred himself in order to keep the gaze of all upon the light source. Because he stood close to the light he put himself in a very exposed place – a lot of light shone on him. That took a great deal of courage. He could easily be mistaken for one with gran-diose ideas – his flaws and idiosyncrasies stood out in relief. Who did he think he was – Elijah, the Messiah even? Was he claiming to *be* the light, when actually he's this wild and hairy man – nowhere near sophisticated enough to have a voice in the religious establishment? But the thing is, he didn't care. He pointed back to the fulfilment of Scripture: 'I am the voice of one crying out in the wilderness, "Make straight the way of the Lord"' (John 1.23).

Thomas Long, an American preacher and professor of preaching, says:

> Because John had a holy vocation, not merely a human ambition, the fear of exposure before the glare of interrogation vanished. 'Find all the flaws you want and smoke out all the vanities you can find,' he seemed to say. 'The meaning of my life is not in what you think about me, but how you respond to the one to whom my life points.'[1]

What a liberating position to occupy. A *decentred* life, where what matters isn't really whether we're seen as failures or successes by others but rather where they look when they follow our gaze and our direction. If we think it through, it's an extremely radical step. It frees us both from the endless, enervating and odious comparison of ourselves with others, and from taking our own failures as the bottom line. The question doesn't even become how John responds to the one to whom his life points (though it's clear his vocation is to point to Jesus). No: the *meaning* is revealed when he can see other people respond to the light.

Of course, it's also a very chastening reminder: what a *dangerous* position to occupy. Pointing to Jesus and the forgiveness of sins, standing close to the light and drawing attention to it, ends in John the Baptist's head being presented on a platter. Such is the darkness that surfaced in Salome, daughter of Herod. Being a prophet can be a dangerous vocation.

Owning our shadow

Carl Jung introduced to Western thought the very helpful concept of the shadow – the parts of ourselves that we keep in darkness because we disapprove so strongly of their violence and ugliness, of which we're unaware and don't take ownership. We can't recognize ourselves in these characteristics, but sometimes others can through our behaviour. Sometimes the clue is in what we get most angry about in other people – because it's too painful to see it in ourselves. What to do? Deny all knowledge and disassociate ourselves when these things come to the surface? Or take them as moments of grace, when part of what has been hidden in the darkness has been brought into the light? What can help us to welcome the light? In the end, it's whether we can trust that ultimately the light will be transforming rather than merely excruciatingly exposing.

This is where the picture painted in Isaiah 61 helps us out. Of course, it's a picture Jesus makes his own:

> The Spirit of the Lord is upon me, because he has anointed me to bring good news to the poor. He has sent me to proclaim release to the captives and recovery of sight to the blind, to let the oppressed go free, to proclaim the year of the Lord's favour.
>
> (Luke 4.18–19)

Isaiah's hearers are returned exiles disillusioned and upset that their rebuilding and return has not been as wonderful as they had imagined. What is there not to recognize in the predicament we now face in Europe? Both Isaiah and Jesus proclaim liberty in the language of Jubilee. The Israelite principle of jubilee – see Leviticus 25 – involved the cancelling of debt and the redistribution of land in the fiftieth year. There's no escaping the direct relevance of the message – don't think we can keep this to soft-focus spiritual succour. If the light is to shine on our situation we can't avoid the economic injustice that's surfaced. And the standard of jubilee law was enacted by the powerful – that's what stopped it happening: they had the most to lose. Laws again need to be enacted by the powerful to bring some rebalancing to our economy.

Switching off the light at the end of the tunnel?

Do we switch off the light at the end of the tunnel because we're in recession? That's called despair, or the very worst kind of false economy. And it's the consumer's view of where the light comes from – a human product within human control.

Imagine switching off the sun so that it can't shed its low winter light to open up the shortest day and to pierce all the way into the place of ultimate death and darkness.

The Lord's 'vengeance' is the kind of language we recoil from – here when Luke quotes from Isaiah it's another word for judgement – in itself a word about as popular now as 'sin'. Perhaps we'd better think about it like this: God's judgement is about the bringing of justice, so don't we want that; don't we cry out for it? For I the LORD love justice, I hate robbery and wrongdoing (Isaiah 61.8) Isn't that what builds true prosperity?

Those who mourn in Zion

And what about those who mourn in Zion? We are very in touch with it at St Martin-in-the-Fields in the annual service for the friends and families of those who have been killed violently. What gave meaning to the lives cut so rudely short? Did it mean that the purpose was all about the cruel ending? In the service in 2011, after the lighting of the candles, the choir threw rose petals down from the galleries. The lady next to me found one and held on to it, looking a little bereft not to find more to take home as a way of holding on to her hope. But I could see from where I sat that there were lots more on the row in front, picked them up and gave them to her. She beamed at me – and I could see that it was through the tears that had now started to come. Somehow hope had returned to her through that service. She had been given a garland instead of ashes. And she started to speak, falteringly, of where she *could* see the meaning in the life of the loved one who had been so brutally taken away.

Jesus, the one to whom John points, will bring the Holy Spirit, will place the light within us – so our decentred lives can be re-centred on the light not just beyond us but now dwelling within. But as Paul – he of the conversion of the deep but dazzling darkness – suggests, we need to remember that we are flawed clay jars and that most often it is the cracks through which the light gets in – and out. Otherwise we might just start believing we're the light again.

Questions

1 Make your own associations with what it might mean to see light at the end of the tunnel and what it might mean to switch it off.
2 What does a decentred life look like? Can you think of any other examples?
3 How does the idea of owning our shadow help us grow?
4 Where does your church have a ministry to 'those who mourn in Zion'? If you're thinking about death, you might want to look at John Donne's extraordinary 'Meditation XVII', readily available online.

12 Letting go

Now among those who went up to worship at the festival were some Greeks. They came to Philip, who was from Bethsaida in Galilee, and said to him, 'Sir, we wish to see Jesus.' Philip went and told Andrew; then Andrew and Philip went and told Jesus. Jesus answered them, 'The hour has come for the Son of Man to be glorified. Very truly, I tell you, unless a grain of wheat falls into the earth and dies, it remains just a single grain; but if it dies, it bears much fruit. Those who love their life lose it, and those who hate their life in this world will keep it for eternal life. Whoever serves me must follow me, and where I am, there will my servant be also. Whoever serves me, the Father will honour.

'Now my soul is troubled. And what should I say – "Father, save me from this hour"? No, it is for this reason that I have come to this hour. Father, glorify your name.' Then a voice came from heaven, 'I have glorified it, and I will glorify it again.' The crowd standing there heard it and said that it was thunder. Others said, 'An angel has spoken to him.' Jesus answered, 'This voice has come for your sake, not for mine. Now is the judgement of this world; now the ruler of this world will be driven out. And I, when I am lifted up from the earth, will draw all people to myself.' He said this to indicate the kind of death he was to die. The crowd answered him, 'We have heard from the law that the Messiah remains for ever. How can you say that the Son of Man must be lifted up? Who is this Son of Man?' Jesus said to them, 'The light is with you for a little longer. Walk while you have the light, so that the darkness may not overtake you. If you walk in the darkness, you do not know where you are going. While you have the light, believe in the light, so that you may become children of light.'

After Jesus had said this, he departed and hid from them.

Have you heard the one about the Greeks who came to Philip, a disciple with a Greek name, saying they wanted to see Jesus? He said, 'Hang on a minute, I'll go and ask Andrew' – and went and told another disciple with a Greek name. He said, 'We'd better go and ask Jesus.' Then the two of them went to tell Jesus and were so rapt with what he said that they completely forgot about the Greeks.

Is this John's guide to how not to be an evangelist? A major theme of John is how we 'see' Jesus. What has this episode got to tell us about how that works?

Seeing Jesus together?

What if, instead of leaving the Greeks on hold, as it were (and we all know how frustrating that is), Philip had said, 'Come with me; let's go and see Jesus together'? Just listening in on the conversation between Jesus, Philip and Andrew, the Greeks would have discovered how important it was to Jesus that they'd arrived. It was the trigger for Jesus to say, 'The hour has come for the Son of Man to be glorified.' They would have heard this extraordinary wisdom teacher at his most profound, talking about losing their lives to save them. They might have found it enigmatic but they would have 'seen' Jesus in the sense of encountering and knowing Jesus personally that John is so keen to communicate. They would have been able to join in the learning community of disciples – and discover that you don't have to have all the answers to be a disciple. In fact that's a disqualification.

I see something of us in Philip and Andrew. I don't suppose they were hung up on the word 'evangelism' as we often are. Sometimes I think we make it a bit like those queues at passport control where the authorities make people stand behind the yellow line until they've seen that their credentials are all in order and they have the right answers. Nothing is more off-putting than recognizing you've been tested to see if you're 'sound' before you're accepted. At St Martin-in-the-Fields, as with many other churches, we aim to 'enable people to question and discover for themselves the significance of Christ'.[2] But can we do that if, like Philip and Andrew, we go off to see Jesus on our own first – and then get so wrapped up in our own encounter with him that we forget to get back to the Greeks? Isn't that effectively abandoning them at passport control?

What on earth is it that stops us from bringing people along with us to see Jesus? Of course it begs the question, 'Where do we go to see Jesus?' Wouldn't that be the body of Christ – our own church community, at the Eucharist, in the places where Jesus is lifted up around us? The view from Trafalgar Square, for example, has taken in Mark Wallinger's refreshing sculpture of Jesus, *Ecce Homo*, and on Good Friday the passion play from the village of Wintershall – very different but also compelling. I saw it with some friends and will always remember their six-year-old being completely rapt. Doesn't it make sense that wherever we think *we* might see Jesus there's a chance others might see him too?

Who are the equivalent of Greeks in our lives? These Greeks were probably diaspora Greek Jews rather than Gentiles. They weren't *that* different. In fact they felt a connection with Andrew and Philip through their Greek names, which drew them to the two disciples. When does this happen? It happens after the raising of Lazarus. The crowd that had witnessed these events spreads the word – and those who hear about it want to come and see for themselves. It's prompted the Pharisees to say, 'You see, you can do nothing. Look, the world has gone after him.' They might as well have said, 'How vulgar: mass revival – and what's the theology?'

Would *we* ever be more interested in sitting around within the Temple courts deconstructing the miracle – asking what really happened there – than coming to see for ourselves or encouraging others to come and see for themselves? John's a questioner – he wants to know the truth – but he's at pains to tell us that the way we know the truth is by *seeing*, encountering Jesus. This is personal knowing, and we can choose whether we take that opportunity and bring others with us or whether we make a belief of our doubts within our religious club that stops us from risking the live encounter.

Unless a seed die

So what happens when Philip and Andrew do go to see Jesus? It would be too bad if I just did what I've been warning against and keep us from the encounter with Jesus. He says a lot, but the bit I want to focus on is this:

> I tell you, unless a grain of wheat falls into the earth and dies, it remains just a single grain; but if it dies, it bears much fruit. Those who love their life lose it, and those who hate their life in this world will keep it for eternal life. Whoever serves me must follow me, and where I am, there will my servant be also. Whoever serves me, the Father will honour.

The grain of wheat contains all the DNA needed for the plant to grow, but until it has found its way into the earth, where all the nutrients are, it's not ready to grow. And it can't grow unless it sheds its protective shell and loses its old life – its very identity as a seed. It's a kind of metamorphosis. As Jesus draws closer to his passion, he gets clearer and clearer about his impending death, and clearer and clearer that it is the only way for him to bring real life. He understands that this will set out a shape of living for those who follow him. 'Those who love their life lose it, and those who hate their life in this world will keep it for eternal life.'

Judgement and judgements

We loosen our clenched grip when we start to understand that we're not the only people in the world, and how, often quite unintentionally, we've wounded others because we've failed to take into account and understand things from their perspective. Just before this narrative in John's Gospel comes the anointing at Bethany, where Mary anointed Jesus' feet with precious perfume and dried them with her long hair. The disciple Judas' immediate response was judgement of her motivation: 'Why was this perfume not sold for three hundred denarii and the money given to the poor?' Jesus defended her, saying, 'Leave her alone. She bought it so that she might keep it for the day of my burial. You always have the poor with you, but you do not always have me' (John 12.5, 7–8).

It's very easy to leap to judgement of others, not giving room for their different perspective. Of course, we can only start to take account of their perspectives and their intentions – which may be very different from the impact of their actions on us – if we are on this journey of dying to life in our personal little bubble, and have started to understand, in Christ, our connectedness to others.

This means taking ourselves and our judgements to the cross. These judgements usually cover up our own dark places – as was the case with Judas. This is the place, Jesus tells us, as he is lifted up on the cross, where the true judgement takes place, and the ruler of this world is driven out. We have to stay with this until we can see it clearly. That's our job in Holy Week – to keep on looking as Jesus is lifted up and we come under God's true judgement.

'And I, when I am lifted up from the earth, will draw all people to myself'

The difference between the way of Christ and the way so often institutionalized in religion is stark. If we continue to export the badness and to blame other people for the bits that are in the darkness of our own hearts too, we might feel as though we're living some kind of holy perfection, but this is not the kind of sacred space to which Jesus calls us. Jesus knows it's time for him to be 'lifted up' on the cross because people are beginning to be attracted to his teaching and living in such an undefended, decentred way. As he prepares for his ordeal, he calls us to follow and to be prepared to see him unflinchingly as he draws the venom and denial, the fear and hatred of the world that this freedom provokes.

As we draw closer, this seeing becomes ever more important because it is in his lifting up on the cross – in that grim and terrible reality – that God is glorified. As we keep watching, the light will shine on our darkness, both our wounds and our wilfulness, and we will enter the mystery of God's judgement. It brings together the justice that we long for when we are stung and hurt by others and see the appalling suffering around us in the world, and the love that frees us and heals us and is given for the sins of the world. As we gather round the cross, we have the chance to withdraw our judgement of others as we receive God's true judgement – and mercy.

Letting go

As we gather and gaze at the cross, we come to a sacred space of letting go. Letting go of whatever that seeing exposes. Letting go of hoarding our life for independent survival. Letting go of our defences. Looking at what harms us to heal us. Letting go so that our vulnerabilities can be what leads us to our true calling in dependence on God and reconnected with others. And part of us always resists it, fearing that our darkness and vulnerability will be exposed. We've already thought about Peter and Paul. Think of how, in John's Gospel, Jesus challenged the rich young ruler about letting go of the power and wealth he clung to for security, or the man by the pool of Bethesda – 'Do you want to be well?' – about letting go of the familiarity of his identity as a sick person. Or the Samaritan woman about the kind of serial relationships that meant she never worked things through. All of us, as we have dwelt upon this Lent, have developed strategies, defences and armour to protect ourselves from our vulnerabilities. To walk this way with Jesus in Passiontide is to tread on holy ground. And it feels like loss.

What is it that we might need to let go of this Passiontide? Where are we clinging on to something that in our heart of hearts we know doesn't bring us life? What's the *Titanic* in our life, the 'unsinkable' thing we've put our trust in, the area we've tried to control, the relationship we've tried to make something it isn't, the fear that prevents us from stepping out in faith, the resentment we hold on to so tightly? Now is a holy time for letting go. And here's a question that the poor Greeks left wondering pose for us. Are we going to make this journey as isolated individuals or will we have the humility to invite others, both inside the Church and outside, to make it with us, so that we can see Jesus together?

The watching crowd is still bringing its questions and not understanding. But it's trying to see. So Jesus takes another image and talks about light and darkness. As we come closer to the cross and Jesus being lifted up, the more the light shines in the place of all our darkness and the harder it gets to keep looking because we're grappling with these deeper places of darkness in ourselves and others.

Leonard Cohen has a gravelly refrain in his wonderful song, 'Anthem', where he growls about how the cracks in everything are how the light gets in. With us it's those weaknesses, those exposed judgements and sins, and the wounds and wilfulness behind and beneath them, that are actually what will show us the route into our gifts and calling. The light will shine on them and through them where they block us from God's love, and in time, as we understand what it means to be children of light, the light will shine *out* of us through them too. They will become portals to help us discover how we can share in Christ's risenness and participate in his glory.

Questions

1 What might it look like to see Jesus together with our friends – and those who ask us questions about him?
2 What is helpful to you in discerning the difference between accusing judgement and liberating judgement?
3 What do you need to let go of?
4 You might want to listen to Leonard Cohen's song 'Anthem' together.

Week 7
'Let him easter in us'

---

13 Standing up in the resurrection

John 20.1–18

Early on the first day of the week, while it was still dark, Mary Magdalene came to the tomb and saw that the stone had been removed from the tomb. So she ran and went to Simon Peter and the other disciple, the one whom Jesus loved, and said to them, 'They have taken the Lord out of the tomb, and we do not know where they have laid him.' Then Peter and the other disciple set out and went toward the tomb. The two were running together, but the other disciple outran Peter and reached the tomb first. He bent down to look in and saw the linen wrappings lying there, but he did not go in. Then Simon Peter came, following him, and went into the tomb. He saw the linen wrappings lying there, and the cloth that had been on Jesus' head, not lying with the linen wrappings but rolled up in a place by itself. Then the other disciple, who reached the tomb first, also went in, and he saw and believed; for as yet they did not understand the scripture, that he must rise from the dead. Then the disciples returned to their homes.

But Mary stood weeping outside the tomb. As she wept, she bent over to look into the tomb; and she saw two angels in white, sitting where the body of Jesus had been lying, one at the head and the other at the feet. They said to her, 'Woman, why are you weeping?' She said to them, 'They have taken away my Lord, and I do not know where they have laid him.' When she had said this, she turned round and saw Jesus standing there, but she did not know that it was Jesus. Jesus said to her, 'Woman, why are you weeping? For whom are you looking?' Supposing him to be the gardener, she said to him, 'Sir, if you have carried him away, tell me where you have laid him, and I will take him away.' Jesus said to her, 'Mary!' She turned and said to him in Hebrew, 'Rabbouni!' (which means Teacher). Jesus said to her, 'Do not hold on to me, because I have not yet ascended to the Father. But go to my brothers and say to them, "I am ascending to my Father and your Father, to my God and your God."' Mary Magdalene went and announced to the disciples, 'I have seen the Lord'; and she told them that he had said these things to her.

'Let him easter in us, be a dayspring to the dimness of us, be a crimson-cresseted east.'[1] This line comes very late in Gerard Manley Hopkins's great poem, 'The Wreck of the Deutschland', the story of the drowning of five nuns. What caught Hopkins's compassion was both the culpability of those on land for not responding to the distress calls thrown up by the emigrant ship foundering on the Kent coast and the poignancy of the fate of five nuns aboard the boat who were fleeing religious persecution in Bismarck's Germany. He offers the invitation to easter as much to those complicit in not hearing the cries as to anyone else – and it's even more poignant that there have been two cases since early 2011 of migrants dying off the coast of Europe, and questions asked as to whether more could have been done to save them.[2]

Hopkins's words could have applied to Mary Magdalene that morning, as the light rose red in the east and she discovered that Jesus' body, which she had come to anoint and bury, had disappeared. 'Woman, why are you weeping?' sounds like a strange refrain, both from the angels and in the mouth of the unrecognized Jesus. But they carried the same kind of message as 'Let him easter in us' – the message that all tears will be wiped away ultimately in the resurrection. Of course, they are real tears. Jesus himself wept in the face of the death of his friend Lazarus. But this encounter is about shifting our vision so that we are able to see and live within the hope given by the greater reality.

Being called by name

It is when Jesus calls Mary by name that she realizes he's
not the gardener and recognizes him. I wrote, in the chapter
about the Gadarene swine, about how important it is to name
false authority for what it is. But in this moment of naming of
Mary by Jesus, and her recognition not just of the timbre but
the tenderness of his voice, we start to get a glimpse of the
power of being named by the one who knows us most truly. It
opens us up to a whole new vista of risen life beyond the place
of death.

The experience of being named by the risen Christ transformed Saul – who of course was given a new name in the
process. He is the one who speaks, in that wonderful hymn to
love in 1 Corinthians 13, in these words: 'For now we see in a
mirror, dimly, but then we will see face to face. Now I know
only in part; then I will know fully, even as I have been fully
known' (v. 12).

The knowing for him is through the encounter with Christ.
It had its startling beginning for him on the Damascus Road
but led to a mystical understanding of the ongoing process of
transformation all of us go through as we gaze upon Christ's
face and are truly named and seen by him: 'And all of us, with
unveiled faces, seeing the glory of the Lord as though reflected
in a mirror, are being transformed into the same image from
one degree of glory to another; for this comes from the Lord,
the Spirit' (2 Corinthians 3.18).

This being known takes us to the deepest place of who
we really are, and as that happens we find ourselves able to
let the divine image and likeness shine from us more and
more.

We might feel tempted, like Peter after his moments of letting Jesus down even after his wonderful naming, to go back
to trusting other views of who we really are, more judging,
condemning and blaming views. But this is never what Jesus

does. He trusts him and helps him to come back to his deepest and truest identity. And he will always do the same with us, if we let him.

The spirit of Christ *will* convict us of sin (and there's another word to add to my list of reclaimed hated words). Sometimes the experience will be sharp like a scalpel. In T. S. Eliot's 'East Coker', part of *Four Quartets*,[3] Christ appears as the 'wounded surgeon' who applies the scalpel to the diseased parts so that we can feel the sharp compassion of the healer's art, beneath his bleeding hands. But it will always be in the service of giving us room to change and letting us see more truly how we are loved and who we are called to be in the process.

Standing up in the resurrection

I want to turn now to that exquisitely painful moment of resurrection between Mary and Jesus that artists have homed in on over the centuries – the *noli me tangere* moment when Mary Magdalene recognizes the risen Jesus, but as she moves to embrace him he draws away, saying, 'Do not hold on to me.' I was on retreat and invited to reflect on this encounter. I didn't really feel ready for the resurrection and to be honest I rarely do.

I thought I had in my head Titian's version of this, which is in the National Gallery. But actually the picture in my head involved Mary Magdalene standing up. I wanted to depict the movement of the two bodies – Jesus both turning towards Mary and pulling away from her at the same time, and she, having moved instinctively towards him, drawing back in reaction. In that double movement was held all the tension between the intense desire to be together again and the knowledge that it couldn't be as it was before.

I wanted to show them standing together – but the only images I could find in the art room of the retreat house had her kneeling down. In fact so do the vast majority of images

of this moment. Something in me kept saying, 'No, she's standing', but I lacked the confidence to try to paint what I imagined,
so I went back to copying an image of Mary on her knees –
a Giotto. Not only was it not what I wanted to show, but
I was using watercolour, with which I have little experience
or skill. I paint quite a lot on retreat, but usually it's 'inside
out' painting, abstract and without any pressure to 'get it right'.
The harder I tried, the worse it got. Mary became a red blob
with flippers for hands. She's usually portrayed wearing a
long red cloak – and I wondered angrily why this was so. Is
it so that the 'sinful' woman is well covered up? In the end,
frustrated by my lack of technique, I made the ground into
a quagmire – I had this in mind because of the fields I'd
been walking through, turned to mud by cattle. That's where
I was – sinking.

I told this story, defeated, to my guide for the retreat. He said
to me, 'In your picture Jesus is inviting you to stand. You need
to stand up in the resurrection.'

That's been echoing in my ears ever since. This is how it is
challenging me: be who you fully are in Christ – don't try copying anybody else. Stand shoulder to shoulder with Jesus as
a sister (or brother), walking in resurrection life. Jesus himself
invites you into the fullness of the life he has won for us, the
other side of all the sufferings and deaths we've shared with
him. Go on, stand up!

Coda

Afterwards, I returned to the art room in the retreat house
and picked up another book, *Holiness and the Feminine Spirit*,[4]
with pictures by an African-American artist called Janet McKenzie
and meditations on each of them by different women – a dis-
tinguished bunch including Sr Wendy Beckett, Joan Chittister
and Helen Prejean of *Dead Man Walking* fame. I was still looking for images of Mary Magdalene and Jesus, and here I found
one, but not as I had imagined.

Entitled *The One Sent: Mary Magdalene with Jesus, the Christ,*
the picture was of (using the artist's own words) Jesus and Mary
Magdalene seated side by side as visionaries and spiritual teachers
sent 'to the ends of the earth' to tell and become the Good
News for all. In common with all the pictures by Janet McKenzie
I saw, there is great strength and tenderness about the figures as
they gaze straight ahead towards us – and an easy mutuality.
The woman who had written this meditation, Susan Calef, a
theologian, had seen 'a vision of the Wisdom-Word that dwells
in the deep of John's Gospel . . . For those eyed to see by John's
Gospel-telling, the image set before us speaks, not "Do not cling
to me" but "Come and see".'

> In the new beginning . . . side by side:
> the Christ, not above but beside;
> Mary Magdalene, not beneath but beside;
> Shoulder to shoulder, two-gathered by the cross
> Rising behind, to one them.
> No more the curse 'he shall rule over you',
> But blessing,
> 'I do not call you servants, but friends,
> For I share with you everything I receive from my Father.'
> I AM for you Friend. You ARE, We ARE . . . Friends.[5]

Questions

This set of questions is more contemplative than before. Resurrection needs living into . . .

1 'Let him easter in us . . .' What can that mean for you?
2 When have you experienced being called by name in a way
  that helped you to know your truest self?
3 What does 'standing up in the resurrection' look like for
  you?

You may find it helpful to read 'The Wreck of the Deutschland',
'East Coker' from *Four Quartets* or *Holiness and the Feminine
Spirit* or to look at some existing *noli me tangere* pictures or

make your own images of Mary Magdalene and Jesus in the garden. If it is the aspect of how women find their risenness that strikes you, Nicola Slee's *Seeking the Risen Christa*[6] is another interesting resource.

14 Locked in and locked out?

John 20.19–31

When it was evening on that day, the first day of the week, and the doors of the house where the disciples had met were locked for fear of the Jews, Jesus came and stood among them and said, 'Peace be with you.' After he said this, he showed them his hands and his side. Then the disciples rejoiced when they saw the Lord. Jesus said to them again, 'Peace be with you. As the Father has sent me, so I send you.' When he had said this, he breathed on them and said to them, 'Receive the Holy Spirit. If you forgive the sins of any, they are forgiven them; if you retain the sins of any, they are retained.'

But Thomas (who was called the Twin), one of the twelve, was not with them when Jesus came. So the other disciples told him, 'We have seen the Lord.' But he said to them, 'Unless I see the mark of the nails in his hands, and put my finger in the mark of the nails and my hand in his side, I will not believe.'

A week later his disciples were again in the house, and Thomas was with them. Although the doors were shut, Jesus came and stood among them and said, 'Peace be with you.' Then he said to Thomas, 'Put your finger here and see my hands. Reach out your hand and put it in my side. Do not doubt but believe.' Thomas answered him, 'My Lord and my God!' Jesus said to him, 'Have you believed because you have seen me? Blessed are those who have not seen and yet have come to believe.'

Now Jesus did many other signs in the presence of his disciples, which are not written in this book. But these are written so that you may come to believe that Jesus is the Messiah, the Son of God, and that through believing you may have life in his name.

I'm a terrible one for getting myself locked out. I've had to stay with a friend, call a locksmith, get to know the *barista* at the café across the road and accidentally watch a couple of people meet for the first time and manage to go on their first date(!), get the bus back to church late on a Sunday night and disturb my colleague Katherine because I've locked my keys in the vestry. It's usually an indicator that I've got too many things going on and need to slow down. And it often slows me, involuntarily, quite effectively. So I felt a lot of sympathy when someone at church told me in Easter Week, after one of our midweek communion services, that they hadn't made it to church on Easter Day because they'd been locked out. Actually I'm not sure if it was locked in or locked out, but either way she's in good company – with the disciples and Jesus respectively, according to John. Maybe it's a recognizable part of the Easter experience.

We're pretty good at doing Lent in the church, with all our courses and special efforts, but I think we're often, like the disciples, in danger of getting locked in or out at Easter, when confronted with the resurrection. It's a lot easier to get to Easter, collapse in a little heap, exhausted, and say, 'Right – back to life as usual' after Easter Monday or an Easter break, rather than deal with the bewilderment of all the different resurrection appearances, the high energy of the early Church and doing the more unfamiliar journey of the 50 days of Easter until Pentecost.

Coming out

There are the disciples, locked in together for fear of the Jews. It's a radical thing they're doing, meeting to share communion as Jesus had shown them at the Last Supper. They're still going to synagogue, but this new separate ritual is very threatening to the religious establishment. Jesus visits them, showing a baffling capacity to be both fully materially human, demonstrating it with his scars – and to be divine as he walks through walls (or picks locks!). A week later the doors are still shut – though not locked by now – when he visits again. And in the process of these two appearances we see how he is forming the Church, the *ekklesia*, whose word roots tell us that it is literally a group of people *called out from the fearful closed place*. Jesus is challenging the Church to 'Come out', just as he did when calling Lazarus from his tomb.

This is a passage that is full of polarities: seeing and not seeing, touching and not touching, believing and unbelieving, forgiving and retaining sins, and Jesus, divine and human. Perhaps getting locked in and locked out presents us with a metaphor for understanding what happens if we can't hold them together, and Jesus offers a key to unlocking them.

'Peace be with you'

When Jesus first comes among them he says, 'Peace be with you.' These are the most frequent resurrection words. We need to hear them too. This is peace addressed not just to individuals to help still their inner anxieties and turmoil. It is not the sort of peace that results from hiding behind closed doors, as he soon makes very clear – though it is a peace that meets them where they are, in their fearful anxiety. It is peace between and beyond a community who are in the process of discovering what it means to be raised with Christ – how that looks in the relationships between them and as they go out into the world. This is the kind of peace we need to discover in the 50 days of Easter. We may have come to the cross as individuals (though there was a lot of journeying together through Lent), but we are raised together.

'Out you go'

Out you go. The disciples are commissioned to be witnesses to Christ as he has witnessed to the revelation of God. It's easy for us to resist this. How will we maintain our unity if we get dispersed, if we have to work in smaller groups, if we don't have our safe haven? But he's not locking them out. The peace we are given helps us to stay in touch with God and the community and be able to go out and come in.

'He breathed on them and said to them, "Receive the Holy Spirit."' This passage is sometimes called the Johannine Pentecost.

Jesus breathes – as God breathes life into Adam in Genesis, as the Spirit breathes so that the dry bones live in Ezekiel, as midwives breathe into babies' mouths when their breathing has stopped – perhaps the most poignant of all because the infant Church did look for a moment as though it was stillborn.

There was an extraordinary story in the papers the Easter Week I preached on this. A baby had died in childbirth. The parents went to see him in the mortuary, and he started moving and crying. Doctors thought he must have contracted hypothermia and his body gone into hibernation. Breathing the Holy Spirit into them is like jump-starting the disciples, emergency treatment to help them activate for themselves the new life of being risen.

We know about Pentecost. We get 'Peace be with you', we get being sent, we get receiving the Spirit – but what about this: 'If you forgive the sins of any, they are forgiven them; if you retain the sins of any, they are retained.'

For John, it starts with this business of the relationship between seeing and not seeing. This is the way he speaks about the revelation of God. To see is to be open to the revelation of God in Jesus, the light of the world. To be blind is to fail to recognize this revelation. This has a huge impact on how he thinks about sin. For him, sin is a *theological* failing about not seeing who Jesus is, how he brings people to judgement and forgiveness by his revealing work and presence in the world. So when Jesus speaks about giving power to forgive or retain sins, we have something in the territory of whether we will witness to Christ in such a way that he is revealed and people have an opportunity to respond to the light.

Light-bearers

I spoke before, from the time in John's Gospel when the Greeks came wanting to see Jesus, about whether we go to see Jesus on our own or take others with us. Then I spoke about the misconception that we have to have all our ideas about Jesus sorted before we can bring others along. Well, this time I think we hit the false idea that witnessing to Christ is about establishing some sort of moral superiority over others, and coming across as do-gooders. Not for John. Witnessing to Christ is more in the territory of being light-bearers – both in what we say and what we do – shining light into darkness, so that people are in a position to respond or not to the revelation and warmth of God's love in Jesus.

When I see those words about authority to forgive or retain sins, I quickly go to thinking, 'Surely not!' How can I be responsible for pronouncing upon people that they are still in their sins? Isn't that taking on myself the kind of judgement I've just brought to the cross?

I think there are two things to bear in mind. First, if our responsibility is to be light-bearers, people are free to respond to the light or not – but by shining the light we actually participate in putting them in a place of decision, of acceptance or rejection of the light. Second, John is aware of people like the Gnostics, who were around in his community – so assured of their own righteousness that they don't really believe sin is an issue for them any more. And we can all have our own inner Gnostic as well as our inner accuser.

Miserable offenders

Here 1 John is really helpful. I had the experience in 2012 of taking the Book of Common Prayer 8 a.m. Communion Service after the joys and drama of the Easter Vigil. It made me think how stuck in Good Friday rather than Easter Sunday it was. It contains two verses from 1 John: 'If we say that we have no sin, we deceive ourselves and the truth is not in us. But if we confess our sin, God is faithful and just to cleanse us from all unrighteousness.'

I always find it disappointing to be confronted with my ongoing failures and weaknesses in Easter Week. And of course I always am. But it's vital to understand that it's our paradigm for encountering them that's shifted. We're still sinners – but under the sign of baptism, under the sign of the cross. The part of us that's been strengthened in knowing the reality that we're united with Christ in his resurrection can take root in him. Instead of being beaten up or destroyed by our ongoing experience of death, we can lovingly co-operate with the Spirit in bringing these failures into the light – knowing that we're fundamentally beloved, not about to be rejected. In its way, the Book of Common Prayer is extremely grounding and grounded. I always find this when I celebrate. It's partly all those beautiful words, their satisfying cadences, but also it's the holding together of a realistic understanding of our nature – though perhaps it's rather better at understanding and accepting the shadow side of our nature than its goodness – with such a clear assurance of the authority of Christ to forgive sins.

'If any man sin, we have an advocate with the Father, Jesus Christ the righteous: And he is the propitiation for our sins' (1 John 2.1–2b, AV). So the Church's job is not to tell people they're wrong – we can all do that – but to witness to how they can be forgiven. Are we going to stay locked in? Setting people free for forgiveness is not just about individuals. It's inextricably related to working for justice and peace in the world – it means participating in the ministry of reconciliation.

Faithful Thomas

'Do not become unfaithful, but faithful' – this is what Jesus says to Thomas. He doesn't use the word for doubt at all. I'm not going to bother rehearsing the usual denigration of 'Doubting Thomas'. In fact Thomas shows us how important it is to move through the different stages of faith to reach a mature, lasting place of discipleship. He's the one among the disciples who dares ask the question associated with late adolescence in John Westerhoff's[7] thinking about the stages of faith in human development. He's the one who can ask, 'Is this what I believe?' rather than blindly accepting what others have said – a perfectly normal and legitimate stage of faith (Westerhoff calls it 'experienced faith') – in the development of children. Is it any accident that we are a Church in this country largely missing later adolescents (and earlier ones for that matter)? I sometimes think that part of the calling of St Martin-in-the-Fields is to be a place where we can catch up on our questioning adolescence, but we are challenged, like the rest of the Church, to go through, with Thomas, to the stage of owned faith, of maturity, where we can say, 'This is what I believe, my Lord and my God!'

In the end, to avoid staying locked in or out, we need to know who has the keys. Jesus is the binder and the looser, the one who locks up and opens up. So let's finish by marking these 'comfortable words' – to take another word from the language of the Book of Common Prayer – that Jesus says to us:

> I am he that liveth, and was dead; and, behold, I am alive for evermore, Amen; and have the keys of hell and of death.
> (Revelation 1.18, AV)

Hear also what Isaiah saith:

> And the key of the house of David will I lay upon his shoulder; so he shall open, and none shall shut; and he shall shut, and none shall open. (Isaiah 22.22, AV)

Hear also what St John the Divine saith:

> And to the angel of the church in Philadelphia write; These things saith he that is holy, he that is true, he that hath the key of David, he that openeth, and no man shutteth; and shutteth, and no man openeth. (Revelation 3.7, AV)

Questions

1 How do you relate to being locked in for fear or locked out of the Easter experience?
2 'Peace be with you.' What does it mean to know Christ's peace amid fear, disappointment, sorrow, anger or conflict?

3 What difference does it make to be a light-bearer rather than a moral judge?
4 Why do you think there are so many young people missing from the church? How many people in church reach the stage of owned faith? How can the story of Thomas inspire us to reach out and grow deep?
5 Miserable offenders – how do we keep hold of what it means to be raised with Christ when we mess up?

Notes

Week 1: God's pharmacy

1 Alistair McFadyen, *Bound to Sin: Abuse, Holocaust and the Christian Doctrine of Sin*, Cambridge: Cambridge University Press, 2000.
2 Alistair McFadyen, entry on Sin in *The Oxford Companion to Christian Thought*, ed. Adrian Hastings, Alistair Mason and Hugh Pyper, Oxford: Oxford University Press, 2000.
3 Matthew Fox, *Original Blessing: Primer in Creation Spirituality*, Santa Fe, NM: Bear & Co., 1983.
4 Julian of Norwich, *Revelations of Divine Love*.
5 Julian of Norwich, *Revelations of Divine Love*.
6 1 John 1.8, Book of Common Prayer, Order for Morning and Evening Prayer.
7 Ang Swee Chai, *From Beirut to Jerusalem*, Selangor, Malaysia: Islamic Book Trust, new edn, 2007.
8 Rabbis Arthur Waskow and Phyllis Berman, 'Red Cow, Red Blood, Red Dye: Staring Death and Life in the Face', <www.theshalomcenter.org/node/275>.
9 Walter Burkert, *Greek Religion*, Cambridge, MA: Harvard University Press, 1985, p. 82.
10 *The Hunger Games*, directed by Gary Ross from the novel by Suzanne Collins.
11 René Girard, *The Scapegoat*, trans. Y. Freccero, Baltimore: Johns Hopkins University Press, 1986.

Week 2: Seeing squint?

1 Barbara Kingsolver, *The Poisonwood Bible*, Faber & Faber, 1998.
2 Adam Hochschild, *King Leopold's Ghost: A Story of Greed, Terror and Heroism in Colonial Africa*, Boston: Mariner Books, 1998. Also the 2006 film documentary of the same title.
3 <www.sarahlaughed.net Sarah Dylan Breuer>.

4 Valerie Saiving, 'The Human Situation: A Feminine View', *The Journal of Religion*, April 1960, <www.as.ua.edu/rel/pdf/rel101saiving.pdf>.

Week 3: Binding and loosing

1 James Alison, *The Joy of Being Wrong: Original Sin through Easter Eyes*, New York: Crossroad Publishing, 1998.
2 <www.sarahlaughed.net/lectionary/2005/08/proper_16_year_.html>.
3 Mishnah Nedarim 6.5–7.
4 See another great book by James Alison, *Faith Beyond Resentment: Fragments Catholic and Gay*, New York: Crossroad Publishing, 2001.
5 Flavius Josephus, *The Jewish War*, trans. G. A. Williamson, Harmondsworth: Penguin, rev. edn, 1981.
6 See Walter Wink's sermon at <www.csec.org/csec/sermon/wink_3707.htm>.
7 <www.helenbamber.org>.
8 *Grimm's Fairy Tales*, London: Penguin, 2007 – or see <www.eastoftheweb.com/short-stories/UBooks/Rum.shtml>.

Week 4: Institutional sin

1 Walter Wink, *Naming the Powers: The Language of Power in the New Testament*, Philadelphia: Fortress Press, 1984; *Unmasking the Powers: The Invisible Forces that Determine Human Existence*, Philadelphia: Fortress Press, 1986; *Engaging the Powers: Discernment and Resistance in a World of Domination*, Minneapolis: Fortress Press, 1992.

Week 5: Darkness into light

1 Martin Warner, 'This Sunday's Readings: Conversion of Paul', *Church Times*, 23 January 2009, <www.churchtimes.co.uk/articles/2009/23-january/faith/this-sundays-readings-conversion-of-paul>.
2 Marcus J. Borg, *Conflict, Holiness and Politics in the Teachings of Jesus*, Harrisburg, PA: Trinity Press International, rev. edn, 1998.
3 See Week 4, note 1.
4 Walter Brueggemann, *Interpretation and Obedience: From Faithful Reading to Faithful Living*, Minneapolis: Fortress Press, 1991.

5 Marcus Borg and John Dominic Crossan, *The First Paul: Reclaiming the Radical Visionary behind the Church's Conservative Icon*, London: SPCK, 2009.

6 Again I owe this to Martin Warner, who picked up the phrase 'dazzling darkness' from Henry Vaughan's poem, 'Night'.

7 John Flavel, *Keeping the Heart*, 1668; my emphasis. Readily available online – see for example <www.jesus.org.uk/vault/library/flavel_on_keeping_the_heart.pdf>.

Week 6: Seeing in the dark

1 <www.odysseynetworks.org/news/onscripture-john-1-6-8>.

2 St Martin-in-the-Fields mission statement.

Week 7: 'Let him easter in us'

1 In Gerard Manley Hopkins, *Poems and Prose*, London: Penguin, 2008.

2 See *The Guardian*, report of drownings off coast of Sicily in April 2011, <www.guardian.co.uk/world/2011/apr/07/african-migrants-boat-sinks-italy?INTCMP=SRCH>, and <www.frlan.tumblr.com/post/16854023638/death-at-the-gates-of-europe-refugees-drown-off-the> for an account of drownings off the Spanish coast in February 2012.

3 T. S. Eliot, 'East Coker', in *Four Quartets*, London: Faber & Faber, 1944.

4 *Holiness and the Feminine Spirit: The Art of Janet McKenzie*, ed. Susan Perry, Maryknoll, NY: Orbis Books, 2009.

5 Extract from Susan Calef, 'In the new beginning', in Perry (ed.), *Holiness and the Feminine Spirit*. Reproduced by kind permission of Orbis Books.

6 Nicola Slee, *Seeking the Risen Christa*, London: SPCK, 2011.

7 John H. Westerhoff III, *Will Our Children Have Faith?*, New York: Seabury Press, 1976.